July 1993

Dear Frank,

A little book to
enhance your love
of the Islands and
its birds —
          Love,
          Carolyn

BIRDS OF HAWAII

BIRDS OF HAWAII

By

GEORGE C. MUNRO

Colored Illustrations
by

Y. ODA

BRIDGEWAY PRESS

NOTE TO THE NEW EDITION

Long and undeservedly out of print, this valuable book has been the object of eager search by bird lovers and amateur ornithologists, chiefly because it is the only book of its type that gives thorough coverage to the subject. The original edition (Honolulu, 1944) has thus come to command a high price among collectors of Hawaiian birdlore. With the upsurge of interest that has attended Hawaii's accession to statehood, demand for the book has increased substantially, for it remains unique in the field and has long since proved its excellence as a guide to the bird life of the islands. It is therefore a decided pleasure to make available once again, in a revised edition, a work that has so well earned its reputation.

The author, taking advantage of the opportunity offered by the reissue of *Birds of Hawaii*, has added at the end of the volume a list of changes made in the scientific classifications and names of the birds since the date of first publication. It is hoped that this addition, together with replacement of some of the illustrations that appeared in the original, will further enhance the value of Mr. Munro's book.

The Publishers

Bridgeway Press Books are distributed exclusively by the Charles E. Tuttle Company of Rutland, Vermont & Tokyo, Japan
Copyright in Japan, 1960, by Charles E. Tuttle Company. All rights reserved
Library of Congress Catalog Card No. 60-15607
Revised edition, first printing, 1960

Printed in Japan

Dr. R. C. L. Perkins

Dedication

To

ROBERT CYRIL LEIGHTON PERKINS F.R.S. 1920,
M.A., D.Sc. (Oxon), F.Z.S., F.E.S.

Who has done more than any one else
for a better understanding
of the Hawaiian Birds.

Acknowledgment

I wish to acknowledge my indebtedness to Winifred Derby Robertson, whose extensive knowledge of books and command of language enabled her to give splendid cooperation as collaborator in the composition of this work and invaluable assistance for its successful completion. She has read my first drafts, made corrections, suggested improvements and contributed choice portions of her own, gave encouragement when difficulties loomed and spirits flagged, and assisted generally.

Table of Contents

List of Illustrations

Preface

A history of the indigenous birds of the Hawaiian Islands upon which I was engaged was laid aside when with the war a large influx of population brought a demand for a more popular work on the birds of Hawaii. No complete work on these birds has been published since 1903, so I have made an attempt to fill this need.

Though not a professional ornithologist I have for many years been keenly interested in the Hawaiian birds. I was closely associated with the investigations of the Hawaiian birds in the last two decades of the nineteenth century, having been assistant to Mr. H. C. Palmer, Lord Rothschild's collector, for 15 months of collecting on these islands, and closely associated with Dr. R. C. L. Perkins during his 10 years of investigation of the land fauna of the main group and afterwards in his 18 years of work in economic entomology in connection with Hawaii.

The several investigations of the former period resulted in the publication of "Birds of the Sandwich Islands" (1890-99) by Scott B. Wilson and A. H. Evans; "Avifauna of Laysan" (1893-1900) by Walter Rothschild; "Birds of the Hawaiian Islands" (1902) by H. W. Henshaw; and "Aves" (in "Fauna Hawaiiensis," 1903) by R. C. L. Perkins. All these works are long out of print.

My work for 40 years was much in the open country and closely associated with the Hawaiian forests and their birds. Since 1920 I have been honorary Associate in Ornithology with Bernice Pauahi Bishop Museum, furnishing a report to that institution each year. In cooperation with the Bishop Museum, Hawaiian Sugar Planters' Association, Board of Commissioners of Agriculture and Forestry and Hui Manu (the latter a society for importing birds), I made a personal bird survey of the main group (1935-37) spending at least a month on each forested island. I am therefore able to connect the investigations of the 1890's with the renewed activities of recent years in connection with the avifauna of the Hawaiian Islands.

In 1937 in cooperation with the United States Biological Survey (now the Fish and Wildlife Service) I inaugurated leg banding of sea birds on local offshore islands and this was later extended to eight outer islands reaching to south of the Equator. One of my outlying island cooperative bird banding associates was killed by Japanese shell fire at the start of the

war. Of course this work is at present to some extent retarded. It is hoped
that after the war it will be much extended in the Pacific and valuable
information thus obtained on the movements of the Hawaiian sea birds.

Sometimes a sentiment appears against bird collecting. But as a
matter of fact bird collectors are among the strongest advocates for bird
conservation and protection. The number of birds taken by collectors is
extremely small compared with what are lost by preventable causes.
Localities are sometimes declared sanctuaries and left to themselves. Under
primeval conditions the balance of nature would take care of the birds.
But as a rule the balance of nature has already been disrupted by man.
So if the birds are to be saved sanctuaries must be under supervision.

The term "Main Group" when referred to in this book means the
group of large islands from Hawaii to Niihau; "Hawaiian Chain" applies
to the chain of islands running northwest from the main group to Ocean
Kure Island.

The use of "we" refers to the Rothschild expedition. Measurements
of total lengths of birds are taken from various works as a partial guide
for comparison. Without knowing the system by which these measurements were taken they can be considered only as approximate, especially
in small perching birds. A bird measured in the flesh by contour from tip
of bill to end of tail, as practiced by the Rothschild expedition, may differ
considerably from the measurement in a straight line from tip of bill to
end of tail as used by some other authors. If taken from a dried skin,
much depends on the system of preparing and filling it. With rare birds
Rothschild sometimes gives the measurement in the flesh as well as in the
dried specimen but in common birds the difference is often greater through
hurried preparation under difficult field conditions. Measurements I have
taken in recent years, as in the imported doves quoted, were taken in the
flesh following the curvature.

The principal measures taken for protection of the Hawaiian birds
have been the passing by the Hawaiian Legislature in 1907, of a law to
protect the native perching birds, and a proclamation by President Theodore
Roosevelt in 1909 setting aside the Hawaiian Chain of Islands running
from the main group to Ocean or Kure Island, except Midway, as a Bird
Reservation. Both partially failed in their object. The first was strictly
enforced, but it could not exclude the bird diseases and insured no opportunities to study or combat those that might already have been introduced.
The other failed in part for lack of facilities for inspection and care. Research work of late years carried on under Superintendent Edward G.

Wingate at the Hawaii National Park will be of considerable help in saving the remnant of our interesting forest birds.

My thanks are due to Major Edwin H. Bryan, Jr. for permission to use his check list of Hawaiian Birds as published in "The Elepaio" and to Mr. Edward L. Caum for permission to use material from his "Exotic Birds of Hawaii," which have saved me a great deal of work, to the Fish and Wildlife Service in connection with birdbanding, to Mr. Edward G. Wingate for responsive assistance in connection with the Hawaiian birds of the Hawaii National Park and for permission to use his foreman's reports, to Lieutenant Richard B. Black and officers of the Navy in facilitating research work on Hawaiian sea birds on the southern islands, to the youths and others who have cooperated with me in birdbanding research on local and outlying islands, to Admiral Chester W. Nimitz, Commander-in-Chief of the U. S. Pacific Fleet, for response to appeals for bird protection on the offshore and outlying islands under the wartime control of the navy, thus assisting in future research work, as well as in conservation of the birds.

For information I am indebted to Mrs. Dora P. Isenberg, Mrs. Helen Shiras Baldwin, Messrs. C. S. Childs, Paul H. Baldwin, Walter R. Donaghho, Fred Hadden, T. M. Blackman and many others.

Thanks to bird lovers are due of Mr. F. F. Baldwin, Mr. W. H. McInerny, the Hui Manu, the local Press, The Honolulu Audubon Society and others for assisting in procuring through the 1939 Session of the Hawaiian Legislature a two-year closed season for the shore and migratory birds. This has now expired but open shooting seasons in the Territory of Hawaii are in abeyance for the duration of the war. After the war the question will undoubtedly be taken up again. It is expected that the Honolulu Audubon Society will take a leading hand in this.

The Honolulu Audubon Society was inaugurated by Mr. Charles M. Dunn early in 1939. He also started "The Elepaio," the publication of the Society, which will fill a long felt want.

In the natural arrangement of the various kinds of birds, the classification is based on the degree of relationship of one kind with another. Thus birds are members, first, of the great Division of the VERTEBRATA, which comprises all animals that possess a spinal column. A somewhat closer grouping segregates them into the Class AVES, which includes all the birds, living and extinct. The Class is subdivided into ORDERS, the Orders again into FAMILIES, the Families into GENERA and the Genera into SPECIES. Each of these subdivisions refines the grouping a little

further, and many ornithologists even divide the Species again into
SUBSPECIES. In the technical names of the birds listed here, printed in
Bold-face, the first name is the Genus, the second is the Species. The third
name, if there is one, is the Subspecies. The name in ordinary type following the technical name is that of the person who first published a description of the species in scientific literature. Where the describer's name
is in parenthesis it denotes that there has been some change made in it
afterwards.

In the treatment that follows the birds are grouped according to their
natural relationships, but only in the section dealing with the native birds
are the orders (names ending in formes) indicated. In the sections on
the occasional visitants and the imported birds this is omitted, the largest
division noted being the family (names ending in idae). Many birds are
known by several vernacular or common names; in this work the best
known or the most appropriate are. used as the major headings for the
discussion of the individual species, the others, whether English or Hawaiian
or both being given in *italics.* Where the significance of the Hawaiian
name is known, or the reason for its application, that too is noted as an
item that might be of interest, especially to those to whom the Hawaiian
tongue is completely unknown. No attempt has been made to include
the technical synonymy, as a complete listing would be unduly cumbersome
and out of place in a work of this sort, and a partial list would be of no
value to anyone.

In the arrangement of this book and in the nomenclature I have
followed a checklist carefully worked out by Major Edwin H. Bryan, Jr.,
Curator of Collections with the Bishop Museum and published in "The
Elepaio," the organ of the Honolulu Audubon Society. To save space for
information on the native Hawaiian birds I have reduced descriptions and
have not gone into detail on occasional visitants and imported birds as these
can be found in other books. For the native birds, Wilson, Rothschild
and Henshaw give detailed descriptions and Edward L. Caum gives good
descriptions of the imported birds in his "Exotic Birds of Hawaii." The
colored plates herein, adapted in the main from those of Wilson and
Rothschild, give a good idea of the Hawaiian birds.

Books consulted are: Birds of the Sandwich Islands, by S. B. Wilson
and A. H. Evans, London, 1890-1899; Avifauna of Laysan and the
Adjacent Islands, by Walter Rothschild, London, 1893-1900; Birds of
the Hawaiian Islands, by H. W. Henshaw, Honolulu, 1902; Aves (Fauna
Hawaiiensis, vol. 1, part 4) by R. C. L. Perkins, Cambridge, 1903;

Exotic Birds of Hawaii (B. P. Bishop Museum Occasional Papers, vol. 10 No. 9) by E. L. Caum, Honolulu, 1933; Familiar Hawaiian Birds, by J. d'A. Northwood, Honolulu, 1940; Check List of Birds Reported from the Hawaiian Islands, compiled by E. H. Bryan, Jr., published serially in The Elepaio (vol. 1 no. 12, April 1941 to vol. 2 no. 12, June 1942); Reports of Paul H. Baldwin to the Superintendent of the Hawaii National Park, 1941; Game Birds of California, by J. Grinnell, H. C. Bryant and T. I. Storer, Berkeley, 1918; Nests and Eggs of North American Birds, by O. Davie, Philadelphia, 1898; Birds of America edited by T. G. Pearson, New York, 1936; The Book of Birds, by the National Geographic Society, Washington, 1927; New Zealand Birds, by W. R. B. Oliver, Wellington, 1930; What Bird Is That? by N. W. Cayley, Sydney, 1932; The Bird Book, by N. Blanchan, New York, 1939; Birds of the Ocean, by W. B. Alexander, New York, 1928; Jungle Fowls from Pacific Islands (B. P. Bishop Museum Bulletin 108) by S. C. Ball, Honolulu, 1933; various publications by W. Alanson Bryan; in addition much use has been made of Perkins' unpublished journals and correspondence. and my own field notes subsequent to December, 1890.

I am indebted to a number of persons for the use of the photographs reproduced herein. These are acknowledged individually.

White tern (*Gygis alba rothschildi*). Parent bird at the nesting place feeding young and holding 3 small fish crosswise in its bill.

Native Hawaiian Birds

SEA BIRDS

Against the illimitable blue of the sky, over the unfathomable blue of the ocean the sea birds of the Pacific wing the cycle of their lives. For them the ocean is a larder: the islands and atolls their mating ground and nurseries. In the air on the wing what can compare with the wild majesty of the giant albatross riding the air currents with effortless ease, wide pinions spread as the bird glides and swoops against the sun. The plummeting dive of the gannets upon their fishy prey, the dipping sweep of the shearwaters close to the sparkling wave, the bat-like fluttering of the tiny petrel, the vigorous flap flap of the booby returning to its nest, and the questing rise and fall of the white-tailed tropic bird against the cliff faces, all proclaim the species to the knowing eye.

First in the most recent classification of Hawaiian birds come members of the order of Petrels. The distinguishing features of this order are well defined viz. a strongly hooked bill covered with horny plates, and nostrils in tubes. The three front toes are fully webbed, hind toe small or absent.

There are ten species that range the ocean surrounding the Hawaiian group, and nest on islands of the Hawaiian Chain, on the large mountainous islands of the main group and small islands off their shores. Included in these species are birds of size as great as 33 inches long with a wing spread of over 7 feet and small birds not over 8 inches long. Two are albatrosses; three are shearwaters, less than half the size of the albatrosses; two are medium sized petrels; one, between the medium sized petrels and the storm petrels; and two storm petrels.

All these birds are undoubtedly surface feeders, the larger species flying all day and settling on the water at night to feed on squids and fishes that come to the surface at that time. Storm petrels generally pick up their food from the surface of the water as they skim the waves, some of them, using their feet to support them and seeming to walk on the water. The Hawaiian species can be seen to skim the surface and no doubt capture their food in the same way but cannot be studied closely as they do not follow ships as is the habit of some others. They only approach ships when attracted by their lights. The few I have examined had only a slimy substance and some little pieces of light pumice stone in their stomachs. It is generally supposed that most species of this order leave their young when full grown and very fat to finish their development alone, absorbing their fat and eventually following their parents to sea. It is more likely that the old birds return at long intervals and eventually conduct the young birds to the feeding grounds.

Some of these birds were found in countless numbers when man first came in contact with them. Their span of life must be very great as most of them lay but one egg a year and at times there is considerable mortality in the young. Many species will suffer unavoidable reduction in this war. When peace comes every effort should be made to encourage their recovery. Some of the species that nested on the larger islands are already on the verge of extinction through causes other than war. No effort should be spared to save these vanishing species.

White tern (*Gygis alba rothschildi* Hartert), from a photograph by Donald R. Dickey, Tanager Expedition, 1923.

Laysan albatross *(Diomedia immutabilis)*. Typical nesting place on "Portulacca Flats" by the lagoon on Laysan Island. Raised rim of island in background.

Photo by courtesy of the Bishop Museum.

Laysan albatross. One black-footed albatross in middle. Lone Prichardia palm, probably the last tree of the ancient forest.

Photo by courtesy of the Bishop Museum.

prominently. The black mark in front of the eye, brown wings and black tail give contrasts. But when it walks it waddles with a swaying motion. To rise on the wing it walks against the wind with waving wings, then runs till it gets the wind under its wings, flaps a little on rising then sails off with wings outstretched and motionless.

Its food is principally squids and probably fish. It seldom follows ships. A young one came to our schooner with some of the brown species but did not stay long.

In the mating season the massed birds make a variety of noises. When engaged in their famous dance they clap their bills with lightning rapidity, whistle and groan loudly. The males fight and keep up an incessant screaming when so engaged. The dance is an entertaining spectacle.

They arrive to breed at islands of the Hawaiian Chain in November, about two weeks after the black-footed species. They mate and build their nests close together, gathering anything available that is within reach as they stand on the nest site. With the mud of the guano fields they build a substantial nest standing about a foot high with a hollow top. One egg is laid averaging 3½x3 inches and weighing about 8½ ounces. The sexes take turns incubating. Hadden says they change every 18 days, the sitting bird taking no food during that time. Dr. Alfred Bailey describes the returning birds as gently pushing its mate off the egg, greeting the egg and talking to it before settling down to cover it. Hadden says that about 63 days are taken in incubation. After the old birds have departed the young ones take advantage of every rise in the wind to exercise their wings by waving them in the air. Closely packed, hundreds of these birds waving their long wings at the same time is a marvelous sight. I once saw it on Lisiansky Island. The entire surface of the island seemed to be in motion.

The old birds are gone by the middle of July and the young follow in September.

ALBATROSS

Diomedea sp.

A single albatross, larger than the two common species, arrived on Sand Island of Midway in December 1938. It came again in 1939 earlier than in 1938. It died, but not before some photographs had been taken and it can possibly be identified from these. Unfortunately it was buried and no specimen taken of it. Hadden in "The Planters Record" described it "black down the back of the neck, white breast, yellow cheeks and an

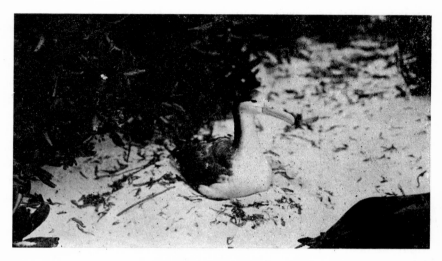

Straggling albatross to Midway Islands.

enormous pinkish yellow beak 1½ times as long as that of the white gooney . . . fully 10 feet in wingspread . . . a very deep croaky voice."

Walter Donaghho saw another on November 28, 1940. ". . . among black-footed and Laysan. species that was slightly larger than the two. It had a longer pink flesh colored bill with a black band around the base . . . the bird was splotched with black, brown, gray, grayish and white."

PROCELLARIIDAE   Shearwater and Petrel Family

WEDGE-TAILED SHEARWATER

Puffinus pacificus cuneatus Salvin   Plate 7, Fig. 2

Other names: *Wedge-tailed Puffin; Moaning Bird (Midway).*
Hawaiian names: *Hoio; Uau kani.* (This latter name si;nifies the crying or noisy uau, and is probably much more correct than the spelling *kane,* commonly used in works on the Hawaiian birds.)

This is a white-breasted subspecies with *Puffinus pacificus pacificus* which nests in the Kermadec Islands and is there a brown bird. On the Revillagigedo Islands west of Mexico "both phases and all intergrades between them are found breeding together" (Oliver). On the islands off Oahu only about 5% of the number are brown-breasted, besides intermediates. There seem fewer of the brown-breasted phase in the Hawaiian Chain and more in a small group that were banded on Jarvis Island to the south.

It is 18 inches in length, brown above and white below with gray along the borders between the two colors; bill brown with slaty markings; legs and feet delicate white with dark markings on outside of tibia, very slight in some, grading to an almost entire delicate pearl gray of the whole leg and foot. The sexes differ little, the female being perhaps a little smaller than the male with thinner legs. The young in first plumage is not distinguishable from the adult. The newly hatched chick is a puffball of grayish down varying in shade from light to dark gray or light brown. A few adults show albinism slightly on the heads, one had the head almost all white.

Its ocean range is unknown, though probably not a great distance from the nesting islands. It nests in burrows on islands of the Hawaiian Chain, on islands off the main group and on Kauai near the sea and probably on Niihau. Undoubtedly it nested originally on all of the larger islands; not likely in the mountains as stated by some writers, but near the sea.

Ashore this bird does not stand on its feet but is always sitting on the ground. It advances by short runs. In rising it hops with both feet till above the surface. It flaps till clear then sails gracefully away. The birds arriving and departing at the breeding island fly round and round the site for a time before landing or taking off to sea. Their habit is to glide gracefully down the wind, wheel right around and sail back against it with almost imperceptible movement of their wings. At sea it goes in scattered flocks flying tirelessly when the wind is fresh. Its flight is steadier than that of the uau (*Pterodroma*). Graceful and innocent looking as the pairs seem while sitting at the entrance to their burrows, they can use bill and claws to good effect if molested, biting and scratching viciously.

Banding has established the facts that they invariably return to the same nesting island, that some of the pairs stay together for several years, that groups keep together and return together to the same part of their island nesting place. Of the thousands banded on islands off the coast of Oahu none has so far been reported as recaptured at a distance.

Its cry is a series of moans, groans, snores and wails, with an intensely weird effect when a large number of birds are performing.

Its food seems to be principally a long bodied squid or cuttlefish, and small fish of various kinds.

The birds arrive at the nesting islands in April, mate and prepare their burrows. They leave at the end of May to return in the middle of June to lay. One egg is laid, a delicate white, elongate-ovoid measuring 2.5x1.5 inches. The majority of the birds lay within the space of a few days. The time of laying on Laysan in 1891 coincided with the laying off the Oahu coast in 1937-41. During the mating, hatching and nurturing of the young large numbers come in to the breeding islands from the sea from early dusk till midnight. Numbers leave at daybreak; whether they are the same birds that come in during the night is not known. But it would seem as if different groups come in on different nights; as evidenced by the numbers on the banded birds. Towards the end of October the young are getting fledged and come out of their burrows. Banding has shown that some of the old birds return about that time, no doubt to guide the young to their winter range. The young leave the islands about November or December.

CHRISTMAS ISLAND SHEARWATER

Puffinus nativitatus Streets   Plate 7, Fig. 4
Other names: *Black Shearwater; Christmas Shearwater.*

This shearwater is sooty black above, darker on head, wings and tail; sooty brown on under parts, tail wedge-shaped; iris dark brown; bill black; legs and feet dark brown, inside webs and toes slate. Length 14 inches. The newly hatched chick is covered with black down which it carries till well grown. Sexes do not differ and the immature is like the adult.

It has a wide range in the tropical Pacific. It breeds on islands of the Hawaiian Chain but was not reported from the main islands till 1937 when I collected a specimen on Moku Manu, off Oahu. A few have been found breeding there in succeeding years. Its one white egg is laid on the bare sand sheltered by grass or other vegetation. It averages 2.3x1.4 inches. The young were beginning to hatch on Laysan in the middle of June 1891. Large numbers came to the island in the evenings and filled the air with their groans. The breeding season seems to be long as I have seen young ready to fly as early as August on Moku Manu and in a succeeding year a well grown chick still in the down in October. One nearly fledged was on Moku Manu on August 18, 1943.

Noddy tern (*Anous stolidus pileatus* Scopoli) on Rabbit Island, Oahu.
Photo by William V. Ward.

Bulwer's petrel (*Bulweria bulweri* Jardin & Selby) in cave on Rabbit Island, Oahu.
Photo by William V. Ward.

NEWELL'S SHEARWATER

Puffinus newelli Henshaw

Other name: *Newell's Puffin*. Hawaiian name: *Ao.*

The ao is the only sea bird endemic to Hawaii not classed as a subspecies. It may possibly have close affinities elsewhere. Alexander in "Birds of the Ocean" suggests that it may be a form of Townsend's shearwater that inhabits the ocean off the coast of Mexico.

Above it is glossy black, underneath pure white except borders of under wing-coverts which are black. The white extends well up on the sides of the neck and on the flanks. This feature makes for easy identification in flight side on, visible as a white spot at neck and in front of tail. My notes on August 14, 1891 say: "After sighting Kauai, a petrel that we had not secured was to be seen yesterday. We had noticed them some days before . . . It differs from the uau in being stouter and shorter in proportion, a little larger, darker on the back and with no white on forehead."

Endemic to the Hawaiian Islands but in danger of extinction, it was formerly a common bird, nesting on Hawaii, Maui, Molokai, Kauai and probably on other smaller islands also. There were 4 specimens in the Gay and Robinson collection in 1891. Mr. F. Gay said the ao laid its eggs in May and June in holes in the earth near the sea. Mr. Deverill of Hanalei, Kauai was informed by old natives that it was a black and white petrel the size of a mudhen. It was not described till 1900 when Henshaw procured a specimen from Brother Matthias Newell to whom it was given by natives who took it, with others, from burrows in the Waihee Valley, Maui. Henshaw described it and named it after Mr. Newell.

Alanson Bryan was told of it and heard its call in Pelekunu Valley, Molokai in 1907. It used to nest in the Waipio Valley, Hawaii, and the natives used it for food. Mr. W. H. Meinecke told me of a straggler that used to come to a cliff (Puuao on recent maps), near the town of Waiohinu, Hawaii, where it flew up and down uttering its eerie cry "ao". It came only at long intervals and was thought an omen of death by the natives. Mr. Meinecke said old natives told him the original name of the locality was Pu-a-ao "a flock of aos," so it is evident that the site was an original nesting place of the ao. Several instances have come under my notice of straggling sea birds returning to long deserted nesting places.

Little is known of the habits of this species except that it nested in burrows at the foot of cliffs near the sea at from 500 to 1,000 feet elevation. It has most likely been killed out by the mongoose on Hawaii, Maui and Molokai. But it may still nest in remote valleys on the north side of Kauai and perhaps on Niihau. By some it is thought to be extinct and if so there are only about 7 specimens in existence. It will be most unfortunate if this, our only endemic species of sea bird, has entirely disappeared.

DARK-RUMPED PETREL

Pterodroma phaeopygia sandwichensis (Ridgway)   Plate 7, Fig. 1
Hawaiian names: *Uau; Uuau; Uwau.*

This is a subspecies with *P. P. phaeopygia* of the Galapagos Islands. It appears to be a white-headed bird at a distance. Its forehead, cheeks and underparts are white; head black; back brownish slate, wings and tail darker; length 15.5 inches.

Endemic to the main group of the Hawaiian Islands and in danger of extinction, the uau probably did not range far from the main islands. It nested in the mountains of Hawaii, Maui, Molokai, Oahu, Kauai and Lanai. The mongoose has killed it out on Hawaii, Maui and Molokai. Pigs and cats accounted for it on Lanai. No doubt the ancient Hawaiians exterminated it on Oahu. The name of a hill Puu Uau, on Oahu, is evidence that it nested there. There are no mongooses on Kauai so it may still nest there in the mountains.

In flight it is more erratic than the wedge-tailed shearwater. It darts and zigzags, sailing between times. Coming in to the islands from the sea it flies fairly high. No observations have been recorded of its feeding habits. Its cry when flying round the cliffs on Molokai is described by Alanson Bryan as weird: "A long drawn out u-a-u, suggesting the wail of a lonesome cat," and other variations.

It nests in holes under the roots of trees and stones at elevations of from 1,500 to 5,000 feet. The egg is laid in April and May and the natives took the young when nearly full grown but still in the down, in October. The natives used the old birds as well as the young for food, netting them as they flew to the mountains in the evening. The young birds were considered a delicacy, kapu to the common people and reserved for the chiefs. The old birds were probably not kapu as their flavor was so strong that they could not be eaten till they had been salted for a considerable time. Taking the old birds from the burrows as described by Alanson Bryan was no doubt resorted to after the kapu was removed.

Bonin Island petrel *(Pterodroma leucoptera hypoleuca)* at entrance to burrow. Showing grass formerly covering large areas of the island.

Photo by courtesy of the Bishop Museum.

This practice probably helped to exterminate the species on Molokai. Alanson Bryan mentions a glossy white egg.

BONIN ISLAND PETREL

Pterodroma leucoptera hypoleuca (Salvin)   Plate 7, Fig. 5
Other names: *Salvin's Petrel; Bonin Petrel; Small Moaning Bird (Midway).*

This interesting petrel is about 13 inches long; forehead is white and slate color, upper parts slaty to black; below white; bill black; legs flesh color; feet black. The immature bird does not differ from the adult.

It ranges the North Pacific Ocean and breeds on islands of the Hawaiian Chain. A remnant of one (head and wing, enough to identify the species) was found on Lanai in 1914. It may have been a straggler, or perhaps an old bird visiting what may have been a former nesting place on dry ridges of the forest in the vicinity. This is the only record of the species on the main Hawaiian group. The specimen is in the Bishop Museum. Caum saw a chick which he believed to be of this species on Kaula in 1932.

When we arrived on Laysan in the middle of June 1891, the young of this species had nearly all left; the Christmas shearwater was hatching its chicks and the wedge-tailed shearwater was laying its eggs. A few young Bonins were in burrows and seemed blind when brought out into the light of day. We found young birds, some alive and some dead, on Lisiansky and Midway.

Descriptions of the arrival of these birds in immense numbers on Laysan and Midway in August are given by Schauinsland, Hadden and Donaghho. Their beautiful flight, aerial evolutions in the evenings, their terrible growling, squalling and squealing when preparing to lay are extremely interesting.

Nature's wonderful plans are astonishing. We can only guess at the course of controlled competition among the different species; how the Christmas shearwater nests on the ground; the Bonins in burrows and the wedge-tails at a deeper level. Also the conservation of food supply insured by the Bonins leaving, as the wedge-tails arrive, and the Christmas shearwater feeding its young at a time different from the other two.

BULWER'S PETREL

Bulweria bulweri (Jardin & Selby)
Hawaiian names: *Ou; Owow.*

This gentle little petrel is about 11 inches long. It is sooty brownish black with a paler band along the wings; bill black and feet brown. There is no perceptible difference between the old and young birds in first plumage. The chick in the down is black.

The species has a wide range over the seas of the world. It nests on a number of islands off the coast of Oahu and on islands of the Hawaiian Chain. In 1912 Dill estimated that there were 1,000 on Laysan. Where rats abound it is soon exterminated.

It has the graceful flight of the petrels, generally keeping close to the water. Ashore it does not stand on its feet but takes short waddling runs and assumes a sitting posture. Surface sea-life is evidently its food. All I have examined had empty stomachs. Its voice is a deep croak, some would liken it to a small dog barking. A sound, kept up for long periods like the motor of a small boat, heard on islands it inhabits cannot be attributed to any other bird.

The birds begin to lay early in June on the ground under vegetation or other shelter they can find. On French Frigate Shoal they were under

turtle shells. The pure white egg is ovoid, blunt at small end, averaging
1.6x1.25 inches. I have seen young chicks about the second week of
August and young nearly full fledged early in September. The chicks were
considered a great delicacy by the ancient Hawaiians.

HYDROBATIDAE   Storm Petrel Family

HAWAIIAN STORM PETREL

Oceanodroma castro cryptoleucura (Ridgway)   **Plate 7, Fig. 3**
Hawaiian names: *Oeoe; Oweowe; Akeake.*

This subspecies with *Oceanodroma castro castro* of St. Helena is only
about 8 inches long. It is of a general sooty brown color, with the upper
tail-coverts white. It is easily distinguished at sea in Hawaiian waters by
its small size and the white patch at the base of the tail. We saw one
on our outward passage on May 29, 1891 the day after we passed Necker
Island. We saw another flying around on June 10 the day before we
sighted Gardner Island. Quoting my notes of August 14, 1891 on our
return voyage we sighted the north side of Kauai when the white-rumped
storm petrel were very numerous. Palmer also sighted it in the channel
between Kauai and Niihau in July 1893. I have never seen this bird to
the south of the group. My observations give me the impression that its
range is to the north of the main islands. I believe Henshaw's mention
of the akeake refers to Tristram's petrel as I have some evidence that it
ranges to the south of the main group. It is hoped that at some time a
careful investigation will be made of the range and habits of the Hawaiian
sea birds, which will throw more light on subjects such as this.

There is no record of this bird's feeding habits and the only information
of its breeding habits was obtained from Francis Gay who informed us
that the specimens in the Gay and Robinson collection were found at the
foot of inland cliffs where the young birds had fallen when trying to fly.
Once at night I heard the squeaking of a bird flying around an island cliff
in the Hanapepe Valley, Kauai that I felt sure was this bird, but it was
too dark to see it. I know of no record of the nest or egg having been
seen. Palmer was given two specimens from the Gay and Robinson
collection where two still remain. The only specimen in my collection
was found on the beach at Makaweli, Kauai. It was a young bird with
the down still clinging to its feathers.

TRISTRAM'S PETREL

Oceanodroma markhami tristrami Salvin
Other names: *Sooty Petrel; Sooty Storm Petrel.*

Above mostly dark sooty slate, rump lighter, wing quills sooty black, light grayish brown band along wing; under parts sooty grayish brown; tail forked; iris dark brown; bill black; legs gray, outer toe with webs brownish black. Length 11 inches.

It ranges from Japan to Hawaii and perhaps other parts of the North Pacific. Schauinsland found a few on Laysan. Specimens from Lanai, a skin, wings and bones not yet identified, are probably of this species. During the "Whippoorwill" expedition on September 19, 1924, when about 9 degrees north latitude, 169 degrees west longitude, a female of this species came aboard. Several others were seen, one the next day, which showed plainly the lightcolored band along the wings. An investigation of the cliffs of Maui, Lanai, Kahoolawe and Hawaii and the small islets off their shores might reveal some facts about this and other sea birds.

ORDER PELECANIFORMES

The members of this order are distinguished from all other birds by all their four toes being connected by a web. Some have straight strong bills and others have bills hooked at the tip.

PHAETHONTIDAE   Tropic Bird Family

RED-TAILED TROPIC BIRD

Phaethon rubricauda rothschildi (Mathews)   Plate 7, Fig. 6
Other name: *Bos'n Bird.* Hawaiian names: Koae; Koae-ula; Ula *(Niihau).*

This beautiful bird is almost pure white with a few small black markings. Some have a pretty rosy blush running through the feathers. The bill is strong, red in color; legs bluish gray, webs black; length 31 inches with the long red central tail feathers, which extend 14 inches beyond the others. Immature birds are barred with black on the upper parts. The downy chicks vary in color; some are white, others light brown with varying shades between.

This tropic bird breeds on islands of the Hawaiian Chain, Bonin Island and most likely it is this subspecies that is so common on the Phoenix and Equatorial Islands. Its migrations are not yet well known. It breeds on

Niihau of the main group and very likely in remote shore cliffs of other islands especially Lanai.

It has a strong flapping flight which it can keep up for long periods without rest as it seldom alights on the water and can often be seen hundreds of miles from land. It cannot stand upright, but has no difficulty in taking flight from a flat surface, beating its way vigorously with its wings. In alighting it strikes the ground with a thud, the thick breast feathers and air cushion under the skin no doubt breaking the force of the impact. Fishing, it dives from a height in the air striking the water with some force. It was found when banding these birds that if tossed into the air they were unable to take flight and fell to the ground with a heavy impact. This necessitates placing them on the ground after banding. An aerial mating dance performed by a large number of pairs at a time is very spectacular.

Its food is fish. It likes the long garfish which it has to fold in order to swallow.

When approaching the nest one is greeted by a harsh squawk which is kept up as long as the bird is held, making banding work unpleasant. A more shrill cry is kept up when in the air and on some islands is heard constantly overhead all day.

On low sand islands it lays its one egg on the surface in shelter of a rock or vegetation. On larger islands it lays in nooks in the face of cliffs. The egg is very thickly covered with reddish brown spots on a grayish ground. The spots are so thickly spread as to almost cover the gray ground; ovoid, 2.5x2 inches. It has a long breeding season from May till late in the year.

WHITE-TAILED TROPIC BIRD

Phaethon lepturus dorotheae Mathews
Other names: *White-tailed Bos'n.* Hawaiian name: Koae.

This tropic bird is a subspecies with *P. l. lepturus* of the Galapagos Islands. It is distinguished on the wing by its white body, a black band along the outer edge of wing, long white central tail feathers and greenish yellow bill. Its length is about 25 inches. The immature bird has black markings on upper parts and central tail feathers short. The chick is covered with gray down. Henshaw mentions a "distinct rosy tinge" and "deep salmon color" in parts of the plumage. Specimens I handled on Kauai and Lanai did not show this to a sufficient extent to be noted. It may have been more pronounced on Hawaii.

This bird has a wide range as far as the Tuamotus and New Caledonia. It has been seen at Midway and 100 miles or more to the north of that island. One was seen 400 miles from land on the return voyage from Midway August 8, 1891. It nests on the large islands of the Hawaiian group but is rare on Niihau. On these islands it is most often seen flying up and down the faces of shoreline and inland cliffs with a flapping flight, uttering sharp rasping calls at frequent intervals. This flight is most likely of the same nature as the courtship flight of the red-tailed species seen at Midway. But fewer birds participate and it is not so spectacular.

Its foods is fish; it dives from the air to catch them. One was examined which had a garfish in three folds in its gullet. The part in the stomach was almost digested but the main part in the throat was perfectly fresh.

The young on the nest have a harsh cry if disturbed. The nests are found in nooks and hollows in the face of cliffs, often easily accessible. The breeding season is long, starting in April and I have seen eggs and newly hatched chicks in August. One egg is laid, much streaked and spotted with red, ovoid, 2.5x1.5 inches.

SULIDAE   Booby and Gannet Family

RED-FOOTED BOOBY

Sula sula rubripes Gould
Hawaiian name: A.

This small gannet is white; its head tinged with buff, upper wing-coverts and quills grayish brown not visible when the bird is sitting. Legs are red, bare skin of face and bill blue, with pink markings. Length 29 inches. There is a brown backed phase which has been considered immature but which I believe to be a mature phase. When banding in July and August 1938 on Howland, Enderbury and Jarvis Islands by taking careful counts I concluded that 98% of the birds were of the brown backed phase and on Palmyra 85%. In six visits to Moku Manu off the Oahu coast in 1937 to 1941 from May to November there were not more than 2% of the brown backed phase. The brown backed phase was present on Laysan and Lisiansky Islands in June 1891 but no estimate was made of the proportion of this phase to the white birds. Young birds in first plumage are brown, lighter underneath and some with a dark band across the breast. I believe they change quickly to the mature plumage. On October 3, 1940 I saw a red-footed booby of a uniformly beautiful gray color on Moku Manu. The egg, one in a clutch, is limy and bluish like

Like the other boobies it flies high when fishing and dives straight down into the water, though sometimes obliquely when in full flight. Returning to its island it flies with heavy flapping flight close to the surface of the water.

It nests on the ground using little material; on Niihau in 1939 they were on a ledge of a precipitous cliff. It is much persecuted by the frigate bird and this is probably the reason its communities are scattered.

BLUE-FACED BOOBY
Sula dactylatra personata Gould
Other names: *Masked Booby; Masked Gannet.* Hawaiian name: *A.*

This is the largest of our Hawaiian Boobies or gannets and averages about 33.75 inches in length, the female is over an inch longer than the male. Its plumage is almost pure white; wing quills, greater wing-coverts and tail feathers chocolate brown. Bill pale yellow, face blue-black; legs and feet yellowish brown; iris yellow. Immature birds are spotted with brown on the back when changing to adult plumage. Chicks are covered with white down. Two eggs are laid covered with a limy substance over pale bluish color, elongate ovate, they measure an average of 2.98x2 inches.

It has a wide distribution in the central and western Pacific. It breeds on islands of the Hawaiian Chain and on islands to the south. It is not known to nest in the main group unless perhaps on islands off Niihau. Caum saw a few nesting on Kaula in 1932.

Many banded on islands of the Equatorial group returned in succeeding years to the same island to breed; no banded birds of this species have so far been reported from a distance.

Like the other boobies it flies high when watching for its favorite flying fish and low when returning to the nesting island. A large flock diving together into a close packed shoal of fish is a wonderful sight. When the young are in first plumage and changing to adult plumage they gather in flocks of several hundreds on the breeding island. The least disturbance day or night sets them off with loud raucous quacking. The female uses this loud quack when disturbed on the nest but the adult male has only a squeaking or hissing sound; the pair stay together by the nest a great part of the time. Flying fish are plentiful near the islands and the birds are almost always replete. The frigate birds despoil them of their catch, though they succeed in retaining sufficient to feed their young. One

Immature noddy tern (*Anous stolidus pileatus* Scopoli) on Rabbit Island, Oahu.
Photo by William V. Ward.

Red-footed boobies on nests, Moku Manu. Large downy chick sitting up in middle.
Sooty tern and other birds in the air.
Photo by C. K. Wentworth.

observer is positive that it always gives up a flying fish to the frigate, retains a squid for its young and a flying fish for itself.

They nest in scattered companies laying their two eggs on the bare ground. The young bird in taking its food from the parent thrusts its head right down the old bird's throat.

FREGATIDAE   Frigate Bird Family

FRIGATE BIRD

Fregata minor palmerstoni (Gmelin)   Plate 7, Fig. 7

Other name: *Man-o'-War Hawk*. Hawaiian name: *Iwa (a thief)*.

Hawaiian tern or white-capped noddy (*Anous minutus melanogenys*) on Midway Island.

Photo by courtesy of the Bishop Museum.

The female is larger than the male, their average length being about 37.5 inches. Their wing spread is over 7 feet. Bills are strongly hooked at the tip, and their feet much atrophied so as to be almost useless to them. The male is black above with a metallic gloss of green and purple on the feathers, long lance shaped feathers on the back; blackish brown below; wings and deeply forked tail black; gular pouch reddish yellow, capable of being blown up into a scarlet balloon under its beak as a mating attraction. The female is blackish brown with little gloss, breast white; scarlet round the eyes, gular pouch and greater part of lower mandible, rest of bill gray; legs pinkish white. The young have head and neck brick red changing to white, probably before they take wing, upper parts brown and lower white. Chicks are covered with white down.

Red-tailed tropic bird (*Phæthon rubricauda rothschildi* Matthews) on Midway Island.
Photo by courtesy of the Bishop Museum.

The egg is white, oval, 2.5x1.1 inches. When the chick is well grown a second egg is sometimes laid, and a large chick and an egg or a large chick and a small one may be seen on some nests. A curious sight is to come on a rookery with males sitting on the nests, a number of them with their red neck bladders partly blown up; once I counted 8 close together.

This bird cannot stand, walk or probably even swim. But in the daytime, at least, it can live almost indefinitely in the air. The night air currents may not be so favorable to it in flight thus it generally returns to its roosting place in the evening, where it *sits* on some slightly elevated object. It can catch fish from the surface of the water without alighting, rob other birds in the air, pick up a small object from the ground if it has fairway to drop down, poise itself over it and rise unimpeded. Only once did I see one settle on the water and to my surprise it rose from the surface without difficulty. It is almost helpless to take wing from a perfectly level land surface. A slight elevation permits it to spread its wings and utilize the warm upcurrent of air, when a few flaps takes it off.

Blue-faced booby (*Sula dactylatra personata* Gould) and young on Necker Island.
Photo by courtesy of the Bishop Museum.

They swarm over every nesting island; floating high in the heavens, mere specks in the distance and soaring in the air at every level, and numbers sitting on their nests on top of the shrubbery. Where there are no plants large enough to support their nests they build up from the ground, robbing other nests for material if left unguarded.

Anything in the way of flesh is food for the frigate bird. It can fish for itself if its prey comes to the surface of the water, or catch flying fish on the wing. The young birds, distinguished by their white heads, are constantly on the watch for any chicks left unattended. Even the old frigates must watch against them. When we walked through a rookery of nesting frigate birds and disturbed the sitting birds many chicks were carried off and swallowed by these white-headed marauders. They take turns in dipping and poising over their prey. It does not matter which one catches it, the quickest flier of the others has an equal chance of swallowing it. Their habit is to drop their prey several times, dive down and catch it in midair. But usually another has caught it and so it passes from one to another till dead when it is quickly swallowed. If a fish, it is ferociously torn to pieces by the others from the bill of its captor.

The large chicks on the nests calling for food hiss like young owls; they squeal, rattle their bills and swing their long flexible necks from side to side menacingly when approached; while the old birds on the wing over the nests keep up a continuous *kek kek.*

Their soaring flight is beautiful and a few hundred on the wing when put off their nests is a sight to be remembered. Several hundred of them join in a flock, heads to the wind, independently, without progressing, they sail from one side to the other, passing and repassing each other; wings not moving, long forked tails opening and closing, heads moving from side to side, they present a unique and beautiful sight. A wide column of these birds half a mile long high in the air sailing to sea in the evening is an almost incredible sight. I saw this in July 1938 on Howland Island. Hadden also describes it at Midway. They would not likely be migrating in the middle of the breeding season. Possibly they were going out to meet the incoming food laden boobies.

The frigate is not credited with flying far from its home base. One banded on Enderbury Island travelled about 1,100 miles to Tongareva or Penrhyn Island. It was retaken there and its band number reported to the Fish and Wildlife Service, Washington, D. C. It may, of course, have been caught in a storm and blown there. It went in the opposite direction to which some brown boobies, its favorite food provider, travelled.

ORDER CICONIIFORMES

ARDEIDAE   Heron and Bittern Family

BLACK-CROWNED NIGHT HERON

Nycticorax nycticorax hoactli (Gmelin)   Plate 2, Fig. 2

Other name: *Fish Hawk.* Hawaiian names: *Aukuu; Aukuu-kahili.* (Kahili—a flybrush, referring to the bird's white occipital plumes.)

This is one of the few non-migratory shore or land birds that is not endemic to the group. It has not changed sufficiently to be regarded as different from the species of the mainland of America which ranges from Central North America to the Argentine.

It is a fine looking bird in full plumage. The head of a male specimen shot at Hanalei, Kauai in April 1891 was blue-black on top, the upper parts greenish brown, under parts and forehead of a whitish shade; legs yellowish green; bill black; occipital white plumes 7.87 inches long, not full grown; length 25.87 inches in the flesh: Immature are ordinary-looking light brown birds.

It is common on most of the large islands of the group. Not common on Niihau and rarely seen on Lanai. It frequents shore lagoons and muddy shore lines, standing stock still in the water with neck drawn in and striking at passing pond and sea life; it also captures some of its food on land. Its food is chiefly small fish, dragon fly larvae, water beetles and mice. Its voice is a hoarse croaking quack. It nests in company, building in trees a rough nest of sticks and twigs.

ORDER ANSERIFORMES

ANATIDAE   Duck, Goose and Swan Family

HAWAIIAN GOOSE

Nesochen sandwichensis (Vigors)   Plate 3, Fig. 6
Hawaiian name: *Nene.*

"Adult male. Hind neck, head, cheeks, chin and throat black, as also a narrow ring around lower throat, rest of neck and sides of head brownish buff; feathers on throat and sides of neck narrow and acute and so arranged as to disclose their black bases; above deep hoary brown, feathers margined broadly with brownish white, rump and tail dusky black, as also the primaries; beneath grayish brown; feathers on sides and flank with gray tips; lower belly and under tailcoverts white; bill and feet black. Length 23 to 28 inches the female the smaller." (Henshaw.)

This fine bird, endemic to the Hawaiian group and confined to Hawaii and Maui, was originally very common on Hawaii and not at all uncommon on the northwest slope of Hualalai, North Kona, in 1891. It probably migrated between Hawaii and Maui and sometimes was reported to straggle to other islands. The other islands did not present foraging grounds on the uplands as attractive to it as the mountains of Hawaii and Haleakala on Maui. It had become accustomed to semiarid waterless country where it obtained the moisture it needed from the upland berries on which it fed in the summer and the rich soft plants of the lowland lava flows where it wintered and raised its young. From being long away from water the webs of its feet had become atrophied and shrunken to about half the size of those of other geese. It probably never swam unless perhaps in lagoons on the lowlands. Yet it enjoys swimming in domestication. The sparse vegetation on the open lava flows is rich, especially on the lowlands in the wet season, hence the birds migrated to the lowlands to breed. Those we collected there were much fatter than the specimens we took at about 2,000 feet elevation.

We hunted this goose in December 1891 on the rough lava flow of 1801, down nearly to sea level, and up the side of the mountain on the Huehue ranch to about 2,200 feet elevation. It was open shooting season and a party of hunters went over ground at the higher elevation where we had taken specimens a few days before. They found a nest with four eggs, caught two very young chicks and shot a young bird nearly full grown. We were not fortunate in finding young birds. It pained us to kill specimens at a time when the birds had young but the few we killed were as nothing compared to the numbers the hunters would shoot of this unwary bird. Ten years afterwards Henshaw drew attention to the mistake of having the open season when the birds were breeding. It is little wonder that the species faced danger of complete extinction in a wild state. There are still a few wild birds and some semi-wild that have been raised by ranchers. It is likely that the ranchers have saved the species in a wild state by this action. The bird is now under protection and it is hoped that those remaining will become sufficiently wary to fight the mongoose from its eggs and young.

The nest is described as a hollow in the ground, or the eggs laid on the surface surrounded by a fringe of pieces of brush. Henshaw gives the number of eggs as from three to six. He described them as of a delicate cream white, averaging about 3.36x2.35 inches. The Hawaiians told us they generally had only two chicks. The two little goslings we saw were brown with whitish markings principally on the under parts. They seemed quite unafraid of human beings. The natives used to hunt the nene for food when the birds were moulting and unable to fly, as related by Wilson in "Birds of the Sandwich Islands."

HAWAIIAN DUCK

Anas wyvilliana wyvilliana Sclater   Plate 3, Fig. 4

Hawaiian names: *Koloa; Koloa maoli.* (Maoli signifies 'indigenous' or 'native,' to distinguish the bird from the migratory and domestic ducks.)

"Adult. Top of head blackish; neck, upper back and interscalpulars brown with rufous brown bands; lower back, rump and upper tail-coverts brownish black; speculum deep purple, bordered with white; sides of head, neck and throat brown mottled; breast rufous brown with U-shaped blackish markings; abdomen brownish buff; sides of body rufous heavily marked with deep brown; length about 20 inches." (Henshaw.) Some of the males have the central tail feathers curled upwards. The chick in the down is brown on the back, lighter below.

This duck is peculiar to the main islands of the Hawaiian group and was originally a common bird in coastal lagoons, marshes and mountain streams on all islands except Lanai and Kahoolawe. Perkins saw it in small pools on mountain forest bogs. Through loss of feeding grounds, draining of lagoons, shooting, the mongoose and other predaceous animals it has been much reduced in numbers and should now be strictly protected by law. On Oahu it is making a bold bid for survival by nesting on the twin islands of Mokulua off Lanikai, and returning to Oahu carrying or swimming the chicks to the Kawainui swamp at Kailua or in the outlet of the Kaelepulu pond by Lanikai. Mr. John Fleming saw a duck fly to the swamp carrying a young one between its feet. Alona, an old Hawaiian, saw a duck alight in a taro patch and three ducklings swim out from it; a few days afterward she had 7 young ones. Some boys caught 14, two broods, on the beach near the outlet of the Kaelepulu pond and then released them. It is hoped that war measures on those island refuges will not be detrimental to them. It would be interesting to know if the ducks originally nested on Mokulua islands or whether they have retreated there to outwit cats and mongooses. The eggs are safe on Mokulua except from human beings, and once on the lagoons and marshes they are safe from predaceous animals. On March 9, 1941, David Woodside saw 5 nests on one of the Mokulua islands. They contained from 8 to 10 eggs. Most nests there have 8 eggs. One I found when searching for them had the eggs so well covered that the nest was quite indistinguishable from the sur-rounding surface. I stepped on the eggs and heard them break and yet could see nothing but dead grass leaves. Moving the covering aside revealed the eggs resting in the down lined nest. The unbroken eggs were taken as specimens for the Bishop Museum. On one occasion an observer gently pushed a setting bird off her eggs, counted them and left before the bird moved. Eggs are white, ovoid and average 2.12x1.29 inches. Mokulua should be strictly protected after the war and the koloa allowed to nest there in safety in the future.

The koloa is an able flier, active on the ground or in the water. Its food is mostly pond life. Henshaw found their stomachs filled with two

species of fresh-water molluscs. The crops of some we shot in Kona close
to grass land were filled with earthworms. They at times left the pond
and foraged in the grass. Their voice is that of the domesticated duck,
the female quacking and the male hissing. A wounded duck hiding in
the pond quacked to her mate when he returned calling for her.

LAYSAN DUCK

Anas wyvilliana laysanensis Rothschild
Other name: *Laysan Teal.*

The Laysan duck is endemic to Laysan Island, but in a precarious
position as to survival. It is evidently a descendent of the koloa but is
smaller, being about 16 inches in length; about the same color, differing
by having an irregular white ring around the eye. The female is smaller
than the male and has less white about the eye. Some of the males have
the central feathers of the tail curled up like some of the males of the
Hawaiian duck. The downy chicks are darker in color than the chicks of
the latter. We found no eggs except a shelless one in the oviduct of a
female. It measured 2.12x1.43 inches. Captain Freeth said eggs he had
seen were generally smaller and shorter.

This duck though strong on its feet is weak on the wing and swims
but little. It has difficulty in rising and generally flies only a short distance,
but one I chased to test its flight "rose pretty high and flew a good long
distance." It is unwary and some that were raised in the camp returned
to their coop every night after being released. The wild ones ran around
the buildings in the evenings and early mornings chasing moths which
furnished food for all the land birds on the island at that time. They
also fed on caterpillars and maggots. In the daytime several might be
seen sitting along the top rail of a fence around a vegetable patch at a
brackish water seep.

Hunters had shot a number when the guano works were started but
Captain George Freeth, manager of the works and Governor of the island
had this species under special protection when we were there. So we took
but few specimens. In fact all the birds of Laysan were given a measure
of protection. Freeth used to send men before the mule cars, to clear the
track of the young birds that had strayed there. The guano deposits had
been built up through countless ages by the droppings of the birds and

Laysan duck *(Anas wyvilliana laysanensis)*, Laysan Island.
Photo by Dr. Alfred M. Bailey, 1913.

dead bodies of thousands of young birds of all sizes killed in storms. The principal guano producer was the Laysan albatross but numbers of other birds contributed to the deposits. It seemed reasonable to protect this source of wealth for future generations. The duck and small birds were protected for esthetic and scientific reasons. Pity it was that protection was not carried on effectively in years following the closing of the guano works. Declaring it a bird sanctuary as Theodore Roosevelt did in 1909 was not enough. Periodical inspection and care are necessary also.

The Japanese plume hunters in 1909 probably killed the duck for food, but when Professor Dill was there in 1911, before rabbits devastated the island, there were six of them living. After rabbits had made a desert of the island Dr. Wetmore saw 20 individuals in 1925. Coultas of the Zaca expedition in 1936 saw 11 but his stay was short and he probably did not see all that were there.

A bird that can come through such trials and vicissitudes as this bird has and rehabilitate itself deserves respect and every chance to perpetuate its species. No further collecting of specimens of any bird should be permitted on Laysan till it is known that the rare birds have fully recovered.

PINTAIL DUCK

Anas acuta tzitzihoa Vieillot   Plate 5, Figs. 3 & 4

Other name: *Sprig*. Hawaiian names: *Mapu; Koloa mapu*. (Mapu signifies to rise and float off, as a cloud, which well describes the immense flocks of the past.)

"Adult male: Head and upper neck hair brown glossed with green and purple; sides of head with white stripe; dorsal line of neck black; lower neck and underparts white; back and sides vermiculated with black; speculum greenish purple; tertials and scalpulars silvery and black; tail cuneate with much projecting middle feathers. Length about 28 inches. Female: Above grayish dusky with bars and streaks of yellowish brown; lower parts chiefly white; flanks and under tail-coverts streaked with dusky. Smaller." (Henshaw.)

The pintail duck is a regular winter migrant to these islands and spends so much of the year here that it is justifiable to class it with the indigenous birds.

The regular migrants of which there are five waders and two swimmers arrive in the Hawaiian group in the autumn and leave in the spring. There does not seem to be accurate data on their arrival and departure except for the Pacific Golden Plover which arrives in August and September and leaves in May. That gives at least 7 to 8 months of their year here, and probably more as they often appear in July (at least on Midway and Niihau). The other migratory birds may not spend so much of their time in the group but even so, it is undoubtedly more than half of the year. They do not breed here, except rarely the curlew, so are technically not indigenous.

In the past this bird came in large numbers to the islands. In March 1891 there were large flocks in the lagoons at Mana, Kauai and in the fish ponds near Kailua, Hawaii in December of the same year, but they were quite shy in both places. We had difficulty in getting a limited number of specimens. They visited the coast of Molokai during the time I was there, 1899 to 1906, and I took specimens at Palaau on that island. I saw a few at Kawela, Molokai in January 1943 and several hundred on the Kanaha pond near Kahului, Maui, where they had become very tame through having been protected for several years by the plantation people. In 1939 one was found exhausted in the surf at Jarvis Island about 1,300 miles south of these islands. Early in 1943 a flock arrived at Palmyra about 1,000 miles from the main islands. About 22 were kept in a pen for awhile but as they did not thrive were released. Some of them continued to return to the pen and spend the night there for a considerable time thereafter.

SHOVELLER DUCK

Spatula clypeata (Linnaeus)   Plate 5, Figs. 12 & 13
Other names: *Spoonbill; Spoonie.* Hawaiian names: *Moha; Koloa moha.*
(Moha signifies shiny, referring to the shiny green head.)

"Adult male. Head and neck green; breast and outer scalpulars white; rest of under parts chestnut; crissum dark bluish green, bordered anteriorly by white; bill black and twice as wide at tip as at base; feet orange-red. Length about 20 inches. Female duller." (Henshaw.)

Like the pintail this is one of the regular migrants that spend the winter months in the Hawaiian group. We secured specimens at Hono-kahau pond near Kailua, Hawaii in December 1891. I collected two that landed in the reservoir at Koele, Lanai in December 1916. There are no streams or ponds except water storage reservoirs on Lanai and the only ducks that come there are stragglers from other islands or the mainland. A flock of ducks which were probably of this species were arriving at the Kanaha pond on Maui when I was there in January 1943. They had been out foraging elsewhere and were coming back to the sanctuary for the day.

ORDER FALCONIFORMES

ACCIPITRIDAE   Hawk and Osprey Family

HAWAIIAN HAWK

Buteo solitarius Peale   Plate 3, Figs. 1, 2 & 3
Hawaiian name: *Io.*

For a long time, according to Professor H. W. Henshaw, the two distinct phases of color in this interesting species were not understood. He concluded that the adult dark phase is mostly blackish brown and the young are also blackish brown but not so dark as the adult. The light phase is mostly buff with some variations; the young of this phase have the head and neck light buff, upper parts dark brown and under parts buff. Henshaw gives the length of the adult male about 15½ inches; of adult female, about 18 inches."

Henshaw lived ten years in Hilo, Hawaii, near the haunts of this bird and collected a large series of specimens of all stages. Perkins had also studied the species but thought with others that those with the light phase were young birds. He had seen several nests in Kona but the parent birds were in all cases dark in color. However, he did not doubt the correctness of Henshaw's observations.

The io is endemic to the island of Hawaii and is well distributed over the island from about 2,000 to 5,000 feet elevation. It favors the outer, more open forest rather than the very dense rain forest. In the eighteen nineties it was fairly common in some localities. It is now reduced in numbers but is still well distributed over the island.

This hawk is a strong flier and rises high in the air in its courtship flights, squeaking as the pairs wheel in wide circles one high above the other. When hunting it sits still on a low tree watching for rats and mice. I have been told it also follows mynahs till it tires them; when the mynah tires it seeks the ground and the hawk pounces on it. The native birds, keeping much to the trees, are probably little molested by it. Neither Perkins nor Henshaw found evidence of its attacking native birds. Both concluded that the io is a useful bird and does little harm. Our observations coincided with those of the two eminent scientists. The birds we killed were gorged with mice, rats, spiders, hawkmoths and caterpillars. Feeding on spiders was detrimental to them, as the webs clogged their feathers and formed in solid masses round their claws and eventually disabled some of them. Only on one occasion when I was with the Rothschild expedition were there remains of birds in the stomachs of any we examined. In that case it was parts of a ricebird. They do kill birds occasionally but during the eighteen nineties rats and mice furnished their principal food. Sportsmen and farmers condemn the bird and it is difficult to obtain protection for it. It should be protected as its usefulness exceeds its harmfulness.

The nest of the io is a massive structure built of twigs and sticks secure in a tree not a great height from the ground. Perkins states that the old birds are very bold when there are young in the nest and are driven away only with difficulty.

By 1923, after rabbits, which had been released there by guano workers, had destroyed the vegetation of Laysan, the bird was almost exterminated. It is not known if any survive there. Fortunately some had been taken to Midway Islands where they have thrived and are now plentiful.

On Laysan in 1891 they were very active, running over the ground through the grass like rats. In the evenings they came round the houses chasing moths. They also ate maggots and even the flesh of dead birds and also sea birds' eggs, generally when broken by other birds. But they are capable of breaking the shell themselves as we saw on one occasion. Moths and caterpillars formed a large part of their diet.

These insectivorous birds are valuable for any oceanic island where there are no predaceous animals to kill them or no mosquitoes to carry imported bird diseases to them. An experiment made to introduce them to cane fields on the main islands naturally failed. Being so long free from all enemies they became so unwary as to fall an easy prey to predaceous animals.

HAWAIIAN RAIL

Pennula millsi Dole   Plate 4, Fig. 3
Other name: *Sandwich Island Rail*. Hawaiian name: *Moho*.

The moho was about 5.5 inches long; mostly chocolate brown in color, lighter underneath.

This little flightless rail which was originally very common over most of Hawaii, is now extinct. It, or allied species, no doubt frequented most of the larger islands of the group. It certainly was on Molokai, where it was known to the older natives in the eighteen nineties as moho.

To Mr. Mills of Hilo, who collected birds about 1864 near Olaa, in Puna, Hawaii, we are indebted for the only specimens of the Hawaiian rail in existence. Part of his collections was purchased by Mr. C. R. Bishop for the museum. On May 21, 1891, we had the pleasure of seeing one of the cases which contained some specimens of this bird as well as the Mamo, Ula-ai-hawane and Kioea, which with the moho were then on the verge of extinction. No specimen of the moho has been taken since 1864. Andrews' Hawaiian Dictionary says "Moho, a bird that crows in the grass." Its voice was evidently a burring sound.

Little is known about the moho. Its nest was seen by several persons in the grass but there is no description of the nest, eggs or young. The

Hawaiian chiefs used to find sport in shooting at this bird with bow and arrow.

SPOTTED HAWAIIAN RAIL

Pennula sandwichensis (Gmelin)   Plate 4, Fig. 4

This rail which is little over 5 inches long, ruddy brown with blackish centers to the feathers, is known only by a single specimen in the Leyden Museum. Where it was taken and by whom remains a mystery. Latham stated that it inhabited the Sandwich Islands and that seems to be all that is known of it. If Hawaiian it is certainly extinct.

This might be the bird referred to in Andrews' dictionary as "Iao, name of a small bird somewhat like the moho."

HAWAIIAN GALLINULE

Gallinula chloropus sandwichensis Streets,   Plate 4, Fig. 5
Other name: *Mudhen.* Hawaiian names: *Alae; Alae ula; Koki.*

This bird, according to tradition, is one of the great benefactors of the Hawaiian people. Fire was unknown to the people, hence they could neither cook their food nor warm themselves during the cold weather. The bird took pity on them and, flying to the home of the gods, stole a blazing brand and carried it back to earth. On this return flight its formerly white forehead was scorched by the flames; hence its name *alae*, signifying a burnt forehead. The descendents of this valiant bird all bear the red mark of honor.

The alae is black above, slaty blue below, under tail-coverts mostly white; bill and frontal plate red, bill sometimes tipped with yellow. Legs in one specimen greenish yellow with a red mark on the tibiae, of another with the lower end of tibiae red running into yellow and green at the joints, front of tarsus greenish yellow with reddish tinge. Sides of tarsus reddish or running from red into yellow and green, and back greenish. Length 14 inches. There has been some disagreement as to whether the differences (principally in the redness of the legs of the Hawaiian bird) are sufficient to give it subspecific rank.

The alae was a common bird on most of the larger islands in 1891. It is still fairly common in some localities. It does not occur on Lanai and I was surprised to find it hardly known on Niihau in 1939. It frequents lagoons, taro patches and reedy margins of water courses along the coast. Sometimes it ventures out on to grassy land. As it feeds there it jerks up its tail at intervals showing the white feathers of the under tail-coverts, reminding me of the large gallinule of New Zealand. Its short sharp cry is also a reminder of that bird's call but is not so loud. Its food is mostly fresh-water or brackish pond molluscs.

It prefers to nest on solid ground on the margins of ponds, a dangerous habit exposing it to the depredations of predaceous animals. In this it is less wise than the coot whose nests are out in the water, nor can it compete with the coot which drives it out. When there are small islands in the ponds it will nest on these and is safe there. The egg is light brown, thinly covered with small dark brown spots thicker at larger end, ovoid, 1.75x1.25 inches.

A small colony of these birds frequent and breed in the open lagoon and marshy ground close to the Moana Park, in Honolulu. The coot and migratory birds also come there. The lagoon would make an interesting addition to the park with its reedy margin and feathered inhabitants. A little piece of nature in the middle of the city.

HAWAIIAN COOT

Fulica americana alai Peale   Plate 4, Fig. 2
Hawaiian name: *Alae keokeo, but usually Alaekea. (Kea or .keokeo* signifies *white.*) It was one of these birds that stole fire from heaven, thereby getting its white forehead burnt red.

This interesting and entertaining bird, a subspecies with the American coot *(F. a. americana)*, has a white bill and ivory white frontal knob on its forehead. Its plumage is slate color darker on the back than on the under parts. Iris cherry red; legs and feet vary, yellowish, greenish or bluish in color. The female is smaller than the male, her frontal knob smaller and narrower. Immature birds are lighter and white underneath. Chicks are brownish with crimson bills. A brood is composed of young of different sizes as the bird begins incubation when the first eggs of a clutch are laid.

Mr. Francis Gay, in 1891, gave Palmer a specimen with a chocolate brown frontal shield collected on Niihau and known to the natives as alae awi. Perkins later collected it and found that the natives of Oahu, Maui and Molokai knew it by the same name, alae awi. Perkins described it as having a white bill with reddish brown spots near the tip and frontal knob chocolate brown. The swamp hen of Australia, a subspecies of *Porphyrio melanotus*, had been early introduced to Oahu and was also known locally as alae awi, which caused some confusion. However, the original name alae awi was applied by the Hawaiians to the coot with the brown frontal shield. In January 1943 I saw a variety on Molokai with a white frontal knob and a red mark at the top end of it, white bill with brownish spots near the tip. There were several of this variety and others with the knob and bill white as usual. These may be reversions to the former type or stragglers coming here at intervals.

The alae keokeo is distributed over the larger islands where there are shore lagoons. It is not on Lanai and migrates from Niihau when the ponds there dry up. It spends a great part of its time floating in small flocks on the open water of lagoons. In 1891 I saw from 500 to 600 on a lagoon near Lihue, Kauai. They formed a semi-circle in front of me wherever I went along the shore, keeping out of gunshot range. Where unmolested they become very tame and are an interesting ornament on the Kanaha pond near Kahului, Maui. They fight and chase each other a good deal. The pursued takes flight splashing the water with its lobed feet as it flies along close to the surface. This action and the prominent white frontal shield serve to identify the bird. It has a short sharp cry. Seeds, leaves and stems of water plants with lagoon molluscs form its principal food. As long as there are coastal lagoons it will survive. Its wariness and system of breeding will insure its preservation.

The nest is a massive floating structure of reeds or other vegetation sometimes 3 feet thick and a foot above the water. It is anchored by surrounding reeds and rises and falls with the water. I have seen as many as 6 eggs in a nest. Eggs average 2x1.24 inches, ovoid, grayish to light brown, thickly covered with small black and minute purplish spots.

ORDER CHARADRIIFORMES

CHARADRIIDAE   Plover Family

PACIFIC GOLDEN PLOVER

Pluvialis dominica fulva (Gmelin)   Plate 2, Fig. 1
Other names: *Eastern, Lesser, Asiatic or Australian Golden Plover.* Hawaiian name: *Kolea.*

This regular winter migrant to Hawaii when with us is in winter plumage, gray and gold spotted above, belly white, rest of under surface yellowish streaked with brown. Before leaving for the breeding season it is black, spotted with white and golden yellow on the back. Below all black with a white line or band running over the forehead and down the sides of the neck to the chest, giving the bird a striking appearance. Length about 9 inches. Immature birds do not differ from the adult in winter plumage. The chick is mottled with yellow and black.

After raising their young in Siberia and Alaska the Pacific golden plover migrate south about the end of July. The young birds follow a few weeks later. Their migration covers most of the Pacific, down the coast of Asia through the Malays to Australia and Tasmania and through the many islands of the Pacific from Hawaii to the southernmost part of New Zealand. They probably travel by stages from island to island. Yet there are some unavoidably long flights. In September 1924 on the 'Whippoorwill' trip two plovers were sighted flying south when about 900 miles from Hawaii on the north and 750 from Howland Island on the south. They may, of course, have come from Palmyra on the east of the course or from Johnston Island on the west which would take 500 miles off the flight. They can, however, alight on the water for short rests. On August 11, 1891, when 100 miles northwest of Kauai we saw one alight several times on the water, staying down for a few seconds at a time.

These birds arrive in Hawaii in August and September, towards the end of the dry season. They find food along shorelines and lagoons which are drying up and leaving stranded along their shores and concentrated in small ponds, hordes of dragonfly larvae, small fish and fresh water molluscs. The first rains bring on luxuriant vegetation in the open country with its accompanying insect life. The birds thrive and fatten on the insects and caterpillars and by May, having donned their black breasted summer plumage, they leave for the north. Before they leave they collect in very large flocks at a favorable starting point on the coast. In the evening or early morning these flocks circle in rising flight sometimes till out of sight before taking off to the north. Perkins saw "two such flocks start from the same point, the one following the other after an hour's interval." I have seen singles and pairs flying at sea but always flying low. Probably they were stragglers from the large flocks.

The plovers arrive in Alaska in late May or early June and set about preparing for their brood. Nest building takes little time, a simple hollow in the moss of the tundra lined with a few scraps of leaves or grass, sometimes beside a grass tuft, suffices. Eggs are four in a clutch spotted and blotched with dark and light brown 2.02x1.5 inches. Food is plentiful and the chicks make rapid growth with little care from their parents.

They fly when very young. The parent birds use every device to divert intruders from the vicinity of the nest or young.

The breeding season of the kolea including its migrations is probably entirely covered in 3 months, while the two albatrosses of our islands take nearly 10 with theirs.

The kolea is a valuable bird to Hawaii as a destroyer of insects. It is here when it is needed and leaves when not needed and costs nothing. Yet it has so long been considered a game bird and table delicacy that efforts to obtain the protection it deserves have not been very successful.

SCOLOPACIDAE   Snipe and Sandpiper Family

BRISTLE-THIGHED CURLEW

Numenius tahitiensis (Gmelin)   Plate 6, Fig. 1

Hawaiian name: *Kioea.* The name sounds something like the bird's cry, and probably refers to its long legs as well.

"Adult. Above dusky brown varied with buff; upper tail-coverts and tail ocraceous, the latter barred with dark brown; top of head dark brown with a medium stripe of buff; beneath dull buff . . . thigh feathers with bristlelike points. Length about 17.25 inches; the curved bill from 2.7 to 3.7 inches." (Henshaw.)

This fine curlew breeds in the Arctic, probably in Alaska. It migrates in the winter through the Pacific to south of the Equator. It was seen on islands of the Hawaiian Chain in June and July 1891. On islands of the Equatorial group in September 1924, and on islands of the Equatorial and Phoenix groups in July and August 1938. It was present but not common on Molokai, Kauai and Hawaii in the eighteen-nineties. I heard its unmistakable cry only once in 20 years residence on Lanai. That was in 1931. It is now almost unknown on Molokai and Kauai but I found it not uncommon on Niihau in November 1939.

Though a migratory winter visitant, like others of this class some stay through the summer and it was known to the natives as sometimes breeding here. Mr. John Rennie, who lived many years on Niihau, told me he once saw one nesting there.

Its food is molluscs, crustaceans and other shore mudflat life. It also feeds over grass land, probably on insects. Its cry on the wing is a *tweu-wit* rather long drawn out in whistling key. An imitation of its cry will nearly always attract it and being unwary it is easily bagged by sportsmen. It should be withdrawn from the list of game birds on these islands.

WANDERING TATTLER

Heteroscelus incanus (Gmelin)   Plate 6, Fig. 2

Hawaiian name: *Ulili.* (Probably from its whistling call. The *ulili* was a bamboo flute or whistle.)

This bird is easily identified by its non-contrasted plumage, slaty color on the upper surface at all times of the year, the underparts white with dusky bars and streaks. Length about 11 inches.

The Wandering Tattler breeds in Alaska, Yukon and south to Prince William Sound.

A winter visitor to Hawaii, according to Henshaw, it straggles in, probably accompanying flights of plover. It frequents rocky shores of all islands of the group, generally singly or in pairs, but occasionally small flocks are seen. It has a fairly wide distribution over the Pacific in the winter. In Hawaii it frequents rocky shores and rocky beds of streams even into the mountains. It is almost never seen on sandy beaches but frequents inshore lagoons. Henshaw records seeing them feeding on grass land. It rises when disturbed with a quick flight and cheery whistle and flies along the shore to another station. Its food is principally crabs, molluscs and other denizens of rocky shores.

RUDDY TURNSTONE

Arenaria interpres interpres (Linnaeus)   Plate 2, Fig. 3

Other name: *Common Turnstone.* Hawaiian names: *Akekeke; Ukekeke; Ukeke.* (Probably so named from its cry. These names are all variants of *ukeke*, an ancient harplike musical instrument.)

"Moderately small size . . . short orange red legs, conspicuously and mixed pattern on head and back, double alternation of white and black from lower back to end of tail, broad white band across wing, and black on foreneck and chest." Young birds have breast dusky. Length about 9.5 inches.

This winter migrant arrives in Hawaii from the north in August and September and leaves about May. It is common in large flocks in upland pastures, along shorelines and around lagoons. We saw them along the Hawaiian Chain in May, June and July 1891. Coultas estimated there were 50,000 on Laysan Island in December 1936.

Flocks keep together when feeding and rise together when disturbed and conspicuously show their white underparts as they turn in air. They roost on rocky promentories on the coast or on islands off the shore.

Their food is largely insects and caterpillars. They also eat molluscs and crustaceans and I have found small seeds in their stomachs. They have a jerky whistling note as they rise on the wing. There is no record of this bird breeding on the islands though some stay through the summer.

The nest is a hollow in the ground sparsely lined with grass blades. Eggs are usually 4 in a clutch, greenish drab spotted all over with brown averaging 1.66x1.18 inches. Henshaw states that the young birds did not arrive in Hawaii till about a fortnight after the old birds and that they were thin on arrival, whereas the first old birds to arrive were fat and mostly males still in the breeding plumage in which they left in May. He remarks the same about the kolea and ulili so it would seem that most of the females await to conduct the young on their first migration. Henshaw lived for 10 years in Hilo, Hawaii. He was near the coast line and had good opportunities for noting facts in regard to the migratory birds.

SANDERLING

Crocethia alba (Pallas)   Plate 2, Fig. 4

Hawaiian name: *Hunakai.* (Sea-foam, from the bird's habit of following close behind receding waves.)

". . . conspicuous white bar across wing contrasting strongly with blackish primaries; in late spring and summer: mixed black and cinnamon back, and chiefly bright cinnamon throat, neck and breast; in winter: extremely pale tone of coloration, glistening white under surface, and pale grayish back; in the hand, lack of hind toe and sandpiper bill . . ." Length about 8.6 inches.

This little bird has an almost world-wide distribution. It breeds deep in the Arctic. In Hawaii it is rarely seen in flocks, more often singly or in pairs on sandy beaches following close to the receding waves. Its food is small crustaceans, molluscs, worms and other sea life. I found small seeds in their crops at Mana, Kauai in 1891 as also in some other of the shore birds. When disturbed it rises with a small squeak. The nest is a small hollow in the ground, sometimes lined with leaves or grasses. The eggs hatch in about 24 days and all are hatched within a few hours of each other. The young soon leave the nest and the mother takes them a considerable distance from it in a short time. They are able to fly in twelve to fourteen days. About the end of July the parents leave the young and begin their southward migration. The young follow later.

RECURVIROSTRIDAE   Stilt and Avocet Family

HAWAIIAN STILT

Himantopus himantopus knudseni Stejneger   **Plate 6, Fig. 3**

Hawaiian names: *Aeo; Kukuluaeo.* (*Kukuluaeo* was the name applied
to a person walking on stilts, or to the stilts themselves. It signifies one
standing high or set up like an *aeo.*)

Black above, underparts white, white running over forehead and about
eye; tail smoky gray; legs pink. Length 16.15 inches. The aeo is a fine
looking bird but odd in appearance with its blue-black back, pure white
breast and long thin pink legs. The young are brown and gray above and
light below, a protective coloring in harmony with the color of the mud
fringing the lagoons which they inhabit.

The aeo is endemic to the Hawaiian group. Stejneger named it for
Mr. Valdemar Knudsen from specimens sent by him to the Smithsonian
institution in the eighteen-eighties. Mr. Knudsen, his wife, Anne Sinclair
and her sisters, Mrs. Gay and Mrs. Robinson, as well as her daughter, Ida
Elizabeth (Mrs. Harry von Holt), were deeply interested in the natural
sciences, especially Hawaiian bird life. The culmination of their interest
was the well known Knudsen and Gay and Robinson bird collections.
Mr. Francis Gay and Mr. Aubrey Robinson carried this on and the Rothschild expedition, Scott B. Wilson and Dr. R. C. L. Perkins were given
much helpful information by them in their investigations of the Hawaiian
avifauna.

Science owes a debt to an old Frenchman at Akaroa, New Zealand,
who taught Anne Sinclair to preserve bird specimens and so made possible
these two valuable collections which have become of great scientific and
historical interest.

The Knudsen collection created considerable interest in the scientific
world when sent by the Knudsens to the Smithsonian Institution about
1887, and no doubt helped to stimulate the investigations in this field in
the late 1880's and early 1890's.

The aeo was common on Kauai, Niihau, Oahu and Molokai; it was
present also on Maui but there seems no record of it on Hawaii. It
probably migrated between the islands as the remnants now existing
appear to do between Oahu and Niihau. Its range on Kauai has been
cut down by the draining of the lagoons at Mana. These lagoons were
a paradise for shore birds in 1891. The species is now reduced to about

200 birds and will surely vanish entirely if not given adequate protection. It is still on the list of game birds.

It has a flapping flight, its long legs stretched out straight behind it. Its food is the larvae of dragon flies, small fish, worms, seeds and roots of water plants. It has a short sharp cry. Its nest is a hollow in the dry mud bordering the shore lagoons in the summer. The eggs, 8 to 12 in a clutch (F. Gay 1891) are laid about May. They are brown with large black spots thicker at the large end, ovoid, pointed at small end, 1.9x1.36 inches. The old birds use every trick to lure an intruder away from nest or young. The hands held behind one's back may be struck with considerable force as I have experienced when walking along on the dry mud.

LARIDAE   Gull and Tern Family

GRAY-BACKED TERN

Sterna lunata Peale   Plate 6, Fig. 6
Other names: *Bridled Tern; Spectacled Tern; Gray Wideawake.* Hawaiian name: *Pakalakala.* (*Pakalakala* is the name of a small fish, probably its favorite food.)

Forehead, a broad stripe over the eye and underparts white; stripe through the eye, top of head and nape black; upper parts dark ashy, paler on back of neck; tail gray and white; bill and feet black. Length 16.5 inches. Immature birds are spotted on the back and chicks are covered with grayish down.

This tern has a fairly wide distribution in the Pacific. It evidently bred near Kauai as Knudsen gave Wilson specimens in the eighteen-eighties. There were specimens in the Gay and Robinson collection in 1891. F. Gay then gave its laying time as May. We found it breeding on the Hawaiian Chain in 1891 and saw numbers at sea 3 days before we reached Kauai on our return from Midway. Caum found a few on Kaula off Niihau in 1932. Kenneth Emory saw a full-fledged young one on Moku Manu on August 18, 1943.

Like the sooty tern its breeding times are irregular. I banded nearly full-grown young on July 22, 1938 on Howland Island of the Equatorial group. Another colony there and one on Enderbury Island of the Phoenix Group had fresh eggs at the same time.

It goes in fairly large flocks, has the flipping flight of the terns and fishes from the surface of the water, splashing into the water without diving. Squids and small fish are its food. It has a sharp cry but not the variety of sounds used by the sooty tern. They lay on the sand without a nest, or among the gravelly coral, preferably where there is shelter such as grass tufts or other vegetation to pre ent the frigate birds from getting a favorable downward swoop to pick up the chicks. When we were banding them a chick disgorged a 4-inch squid in an open space and a frigate dipped down and secured it. They were dipping at the disturbed chicks but did not catch any while we were there. The chicks sought the grass tufts for shelter after being banded. A fresh egg taken the same day, July 23, 1938, was ovoid, thickly covered with small dark brown and smaller purplish spots thicker at the large end, 1.75x1.25 inches: a very neat looking egg. I once saw several attacking a curlew, recognizing it as an egg stealer. They attacked it from the air while it was on the ground and the terns seemed to have considerable advantage.

SOOTY TERN

Sterna fuscata oahuensis Bloxam

Hawaiian name: *Ewaewa*. (The name signifies "to make one uncomfortable," evidently because of the incessant screeching cries of the birds.)

Forehead, sides of head and all under parts white. Upper parts sooty brown or almost black; long forked tail outer feathers of which are marked with white; bill and legs black. Length 16.5 inches. Immature birds are brown, under parts lighter, upper parts spotted with white caused by many of the feathers having white tips. Chicks are spotted gray and brown; when very young the down is stuck together in bunches giving the appearance of the tips being wet; protective coloring is thus almost perfect as the bird lies flat and perfectly still in the sand.

The sooty tern has a wide range over the world. Our subspecies probably reaches to Samoa. On Rose Atoll near Samoa on August 4, 1938 an immense flock of immature and old birds, all in full plumage, were packed on the ground under the pisonia trees. I found it everywhere I went on the Hawaiian Chain, the Equatorial and Phoenix Islands. A large flock breeds on Moku Manu off the Oahu coast. They can often be heard calling at night when approaching the islands. Their breeding habits are different from those of the gray-backed tern though the site chosen is much the same. A flock starts to lay, another takes up where they left off and so on till there is a belt of tern eggs and young half a mile long with full-grown chicks at one end and eggs just hatching at the other, or fair-sized chicks at one end and birds laying at the other. The noise

Sooty tern *(Sterna fuscata oahuensis)* nesting on Moku Manu.
Photo by C. K. Wentworth.

they make is tremendous, a series of screams and yells kept up night and day, especially at the laying end of the belt. When they come to a nesting island they do not land at once. On some islands they come after dark and leave before daybreak. On Howland Island in 1924 I had to go out in the night and knock down a specimen before I could tell which species was making the nightly din.

NECKER ISLAND TERN

Procelsterna cerulea saxatilis Fisher

Other names: *Little Gray Tern; Blue-gray Tern.*

This neat little bird is gray all over, with some little differences in shade and very little white on the wings.

E. H. Bryan lists this bird as being at Marcus, Kaula and Johnston Islands. We did not collect it on the Rothschild expedition along the Hawaiian Chain in 1891. We saw it only at Nihoa on the way out and after we sighted Kauai on the return trip. Caum reported a small colony on Kaula in 1932. It was present at Howland Island on the Whippoorwill trip in 1924 and a bander reported it as there in 1940, but he failed to catch and band any. It or *P. c. cerulea* was also on Enderbury Island in 1939 but James Kinney who was banding there found it so hard to catch that he succeeded in banding only one. On Howland Island in 1924 they could be knocked down with the hand, they flew so close, somewhat resembling the action of the white tern. It is familiar yet wary. I failed to find their nesting place though it must have been close at hand. Had time permitted I might have found nests, but our stay was short.

NODDY TERN

Anous stolidus pileatus (Scopoli)   Plate 6, Fig. 4
Hawaiian name: *Noio koha.* (According to Francis Gay (1891) the name is probably a shortened form of *Noio kohaha*, the large *noio.*)

Forehead and top of head light gray; body sooty brown, almost black on wings and tail. Bill black; feet blackish brown. The immature bird is much the same in color as the adult but the gray does not reach the top of the head. The chick is covered with light gray down when hatched and afterwards turns black. They vary from almost white through gray, light brown and dark brown to almost black. Length about 15 inches.

The noddy was nearly everywhere on the Hawaiian Chain in 1891 but not in large numbers; on Howland Island in 1924; on most of the islands visited by the Taney expedition in 1938. However, I have seen it nowhere in such numbers as on Manana or Rabbit Island off the coast of Oahu. It is also in fair numbers on Moku Manu and Mokulea off Mokapu, Oahu. My Hawaiian friend, Alona, who has lived since a youth at Waimanalo, says there were none on Manana forty years ago and he knew no Hawaiian name for it. During the Rothschild expedition, 1890 to 1893, and during Perkins' collecting period, 1892 to 1902, I never heard of sea birds on islands off the coast of Oahu. They had probably been exterminated by the ancient Hawaiians and have gradually worked their way back.

The wing action is not so quick as that of the sooty tern. Its food is fish and squids. Its voice is an *eyeak* which it keeps up night and day at the nesting island. On the sand islands it nests on the sand, in tufts of grass, among stones; on Manana the eggs are laid on the bare rock about 3 feet apart. At Swain's Island in the Union group in 1938 they had well-grown young in the tops of high coconut trees, safe from the pigs which roamed the island. In the early part of the season in March before they start to lay, they come to the island at dark and leave at daybreak. Clutch one, ovoid, 2.2x1.5 inches; dark gray with large brown spots and blotches thicker at the large end. A large egg compared with those of the sooty and gray-backed terns.

HAWAIIAN TERN

Anous minutus melanogenys Gray   Plate 6, Fig. 5

Other name: *Hawaiian Noddy.* Hawaiian names: *Noio; Lae hina.* (Referring to its gray *(hina)* forehead.)

More gray on the head than the noddy, body color darker, lighter above tail and legs lighter. (Laysan 1891) Length 14 inches.

We collected this bird first at Hanakapiai, Kauai in April 1891 where the birds were nesting in a cave. Rothschild named it as new, *Anous hawaiiensis.* We found it on most of the islands of the Hawaiian Chain. It was on islands of the Equatorial and Phoenix groups in 1924 and 1938. It is the only tern that stays round the coast of the main islands of the Hawaiian group. In fact it is the only sea bird to do so; the others feed at sea. I have seen a group of noio fishing where the sea was breaking on rocks, when the wave receded they splashed into the smooth water and cleverly evaded the incoming breakers. Their food is probably mostly small shoreside fish. Small flocks follow fishing boats to pick up small fish thrown on the water to attract large fish. Their cry is shriller than that of the noddy, more like the sooty tern's ordinary cry. On the coasts of the main group it nests in nooks and ledges in caves in the cliffs. On the low sand islands it builds a nest of green leaves in trees, if any, or on the top of any shrubs available. The same nest used from year to year becomes a solid little block. The chicks are gentle creatures. One egg is laid, ovoid, light gray with reddish spots, bright and variously shaded, 1.75x1.25 inches.

WHITE TERN

Gygis alba rothschildi Hartert

Other names: *Fairy Tern; Love Tern.* Hawaiian name: *Manuoku.* (F. Gay, 1891.)

All pure white except black ring round eye and light brown shafts of primaries; large black eyes; bill black with blue base; legs and toes light blue, webs white, claws black. Length 13.25 inches. Immature birds are gray; chicks are yellowish white with dark spots.

feeding and the habit of starting to incubate while laying favors this increase. Some probably migrate to the infested region.

It was a common bird in the eighteen-nineties, but so many of its hunting grounds have been taken up for agriculture that its numbers have decreased. Sportsmen and farmers also probably kill it for its fancied depredations on game and poultry. As a matter of fact it is a valuable bird and should be protected. Its food is almost wholly mice which it kills in large numbers. Nests can be seen with several well fed chicks, all of different sizes, and several freshly killed mice lying around them. On Lanai some hunted over the trees in the small forest, searching for birds' nests, but the birds took precautions to hide their nests from them. A young crippled owl unable to fly became quite tame. It wandered at large but came regularly to the kitchen to demand food. On approach of a dog or cat it spread out its wings till only the wings, eyes and bill showed in front, giving it a menacing appearance. Dogs and cats feared its sharp claws which it did not hesitate to use if they came within reach of its spring.

It has several cries. The young make a hissing sound. The old birds have a sound like a muffled dog bark. It nests in grass tufts in a hollow in the earth. The eggs are white and almost round.

FOREST BIRDS

Bird collecting in the Hawaiian forests requires stamina. The collector must be hardy, patient and adventurous, for the pursuit of bird specimens will require all these qualities—and more.

This was particularly true fifty years ago, where much primeval jungle still existed unbroken by cattle trails, imposing an impenetrable thicket to the hunter.

The outer fringes of the forest were open, beginning as they did on the lower and more arid districts where the undergrowth had been thinned by the encroachment of cattle and pigs. These open forests were the collector's paradise.

The widely spaced trees and open glades made a charming scene. The sunlight falls in a tapestry of broken light and shade against which the birds flash in bright colors, with quick flight and cheerful song. The woods are full of sound and movement as the birds in great numbers flit among the branches in search of food.

Moving on into the forest conditions change and become more difficult. Trees increase, the perspective narrows, shadows darken, footing is less secure and moisture, fog and mist increase. The birds seem to reflect their environment. They are perpetually shaking the rain drops from their feathers as they slip about under the protecting canopy of leaves and vines.

Finally the innermost fastnesses of the mountain forest are reached. Here is the continuous drip, drip, drip, of the rain forest; aerial roots, creepers, tangled vines, fallen trees raise the floor of the forest and afford treacherous footing. Moss clothes the trees, ferns cling to rotting trunks, lianes web the branches in tough embrace. Below are mud, mire and bog, and often lava cracks and holes. Nor is this level country. Steep palis drop into abrupt ravines to imperil life and limb. Vagrant drifts of fog forever wind and twist among the spectral trees. Hours may pass without sight of birds and disappointment add further depression to the melancholy scene.

To find a rare bird after days of wet camps, floundering marches and constant peering is rich reward well earned by personal hardihood.

Such well describes what Wilson, Rothschild's collectors, Perkins and Henshaw experienced when studying the Hawaiian birds in the 1880's and 1890's, Perkins especially, as he spent fully four years and a half of time actually in the forests, sometimes confined to his tent for days at a time by the pouring rain.

Since civilization came to the Hawaiian islands the experience of the native perching birds has been tragic. Early voyagers found the birds plentiful on Oahu. In the eighteen nineties the birds of Oahu were much reduced and some were extinct or almost so. They were then still numerous on the other islands. Later this reduction was experienced on the other islands in turn. My conclusions after the survey (1936-1937) were that 25 species had a fair chance of survival while 30 species were gone or likely to become entirely extinct. Many reasons have been given for this reduction by writers, but the main reason in most cases in my opinion has been the introduction of diseases such as bird malaria and bird sleeping sickness, wherever human population increased. In 1934 I found that the first had been found in birds in Fiji and the latter in birds in New Zealand. In 1938 Dr. Joseph E. Alicata found pigeon malaria in pigeons in Honolulu ("Hawaii Farm and Home" April 15, 1938). And in 1941 two species of bird malaria were found in introduced birds in the Hawaii National Park. (Report of Paul H. Baldwin to the Superintendent dated August 2, 1941.)

Quoting from my report of December 1937: "Of course it is possible that some of the birds that I think will disappear may hold on for some time and some may even increase again. But judging from past experience I much doubt if any of them will do so or even eventually survive. I think we shall be fortunate if we can save all of the first list and have them increase to anything like their former numbers." An investigation undertaken in the Hawaii National Park under Edward G. Wingate, Superintendent, (a result of this survey) opens up a new prospect of survival for the Hawaiian forest birds.

As a contrast to the condition described I quote from Dr. R. C. L. Perkins: "When I first arrived in Kona the great ohia trees at an elevation of 2,500 feet were a mass of bloom and each of them was literally alive with hordes of crimson apapane and scarlet iiwi, while, continually crossing from the top of one great tree to another, the oo could be seen on the wing sometimes six or eight at a time.

The amakihi was numerous in the same trees but less conspicuous and occasionally one of the long billed Hemignathus. Feeding on the fruit of the ieie could be seen the Hawaiian crow commonly and the ou in great abundance. The picture of this noisy, active and often quarrelsome assembly of birds many of them of brilliant colors was one never to be forgotten. After the flowering of the ohia was over the great gathering naturally dispersed, but even then the bird population was very great."

This refers to 1892. Perkins found in 1894 a very different condition. A mild boom in coffee growing had much increased the human population, and the bird population had decreased. In 1891 when the Rothschild expedition was collecting in the same region Perkins here refers to, the birds were very numerous. The ohia trees were not flowering but the ieie vine provided food, not from nectar but from the pulpy bracts of its plentiful flowers.

ORDER PASSERIFORMES

CORVIDAE   Crow Family

HAWAIIAN CROW

Corvus tropicus Gmelin   Plate 8, Fig. 7

Hawaiian name: *Alala*. (This name may have either of two derivations, both very appropriate. *Alala* is to cry like a young animal; the call of the crow at times resembles the cry of a child. Also, *ala*, to rise up, and *la*, the sun, hence, to arise with the sun; the crows made a great noise in the early morning.)

Plumage dark brown, head and tail almost black; bill, legs and feet black; iris brown. Length 21 inches. There is little difference between males and females. Immature birds are a little lighter in color than the adults and have light blue eyes.

Endemic to the island of Hawaii and there confined to the Kona side from Kau to Puuwaawaa where it was numerous in the eighteen-nineties. It inhabited forest and open country from 1,000 to 8,000 feet elevation. It flew above the tree tops and frequented the vegetation from the highest trees to the ground. Perkins was puzzled to account for its being confined to this area when there was so much additional country suitable to it. The bird survey (1936-37) found it still in the Kau and Puuwaawaa forests but in greatly reduced numbers.

In flight their wing movement may be loud and noisy or, again entirely silent as they sail from tree to tree on motionless wings.

When we were in Kona in 1891 the alala was numerous. They went in flocks and were most inquisitive, following the intruder with loud cawing. The least imitation of their cry brought them close in. We saw an amusing instance of this. A tethered horse on the mountain of Hualalai, neighing for company brought a whole flock down around it. This trait has no doubt been exploited to their undoing. In the early 1890's as Kona became more closely settled the farmers, exasperated by the depredations of the crows in feed pens and poultry yards, made war on it, capitalizing on its well known traits of curiosity. By imitating its call many birds would easily be brought to gun. Years later when on the bird survey in 1937, I found a great change. The birds were greatly reduced in numbers. I saw no flocks, only a few scattered individuals. The birds refused to answer my call, perhaps having learned the danger of it, thus proving the "sagacity of the crow."

Their food was originally largely the fleshy flower bracts and ripe fruit of the ieie vine *(Freycinetia arborea)*, the berry of the ohelo and other berries. The ieie was very common and flowered and fruited at different elevations at different seasons, so furnished food most of the year. Later as the country developed and new fruits and livestock were introduced, their food habits changed to include the imported berries and carrion of dead animals.

The antics of the crow furnish no end of entertainment. One, wounded and kept captive proved the source of much interest. It was gentle from the first and did not attempt to bite. His food was meat, raw or cooked, boiled rice, etc. It held the meat with its foot while eating and was not greedy.

Its call is a harsh caw repeated rapidly. A flock calling in unison made a great hubbub. It was the noisest bird in the lower Kona forests at daybreak. The nest is of rough sticks lined with finer material. There seems to be no record of eggs or chicks.

The crow has been accused of robbing other birds' nests but in 1891 it did not affect the small birds to any extent as they were very numerous.

The Hawaiians snared the crow and used the black feathers for kahilis and for dressing idols.

It should have protection for its interest as an endemic bird, and its potential entertainment value.

MUSCICAPIDAE   Thrush, Warbler and Flycatcher Family

Muscicapidae is divided into various subfamilies, formerly known as families, such as Turdinae, the thrushes, Sylviinae, the warblers, Muscicapinae, the old world flycatchers.

The Hawaiian Thrushes

The different species of the genus Phaeornis, the Hawaiian thrushes, were common on Hawaii, Kauai, Molokai and Lanai during the 1890's except the small *P. palmeri* of Kauai, which was rare. The species of Oahu and Maui had entirely disappeared and no specimen of either exists today. On the islands first mentioned the different species have since been much reduced in numbers and have entirely disappeared from localities where formerly they were common. This decrease took place at different times on the different islands.

The species were known by different names on different islands, as kamao, omau, olomao. Perkins thinks these are corruptions of the name Amaui, shortened from Manu-a-Maui, the bird of the demigod Maui. He thought its fine song justified that rank. Dole in 1879 calls it Amaui and Bloxam in 1825 calls it Amauee. Mr. F. Gay informed us that the Kauai thrush had two names but gave us only one, kamao. In regard to a Phaeornis formerly inhabiting Maui Perkins says: "I was assured by a native who was familiar with the birds that years ago the amaui was abundant in the Iao Valley. He particularly mentioned and described the song."

The large species are to a great extent frugivorous, feeding on the fruit and berries of various forest trees and shrubs.

The Kauai, Molokai, Hawaii and Oahu species were fine singers, the small *P. palmeri* is also a singer but the Lanai bird has only two or three notes which it uses constantly. All except the Molokai and Lanai species like to sing from the topmost branch of a dead tree. Perkins says: "The song of the Hawaii thrush surpasses in beauty that of all other native birds . . . It will sing at intervals during the whole day, and day after day from the same tree and even from the selfsame bough." He mentions "The wild outburst of song which the Amaui pours forth on the wing as it descends from a lofty tree to lower cover, can hardly fail to strike the attention of anyone who wanders through the forest." When I was with Palmer on Hawaii from September 1891 to February 1892, the amaui of Hawaii did not impress us as a singer as much as the amaui of Kauai; perhaps not so much as to the quality of its song as that it did not seem so lavish of it as the Kauai species. The members of the genus Phaeornis were of great value as distributors of the forest trees. They swallow the berries whole and scatter the seed over the forest.

All the species have a habit of quivering their wings and trembling their bodies when approached or affected by any excitement. Perkins thinks it is from fear, Henshaw thought not. I agree with Henshaw as I particularly noted in 1936 when one was singing on the top of a high dead tree at Kaholuamanu, Kauai. I was well hidden in the brushwood and am sure the bird could not see me or know of my presence. It trembled its wings between songs.

The native thrush can be distinguished from the imported Hwa-mei (*Trochalopterum canorum*), which has penetrated to the depths of the Hawaiian forests, by its flight when disturbed: the imported bird dives down into the brushwood, and the native flies upward into the trees.

HAWAII THRUSH

Phaeornis obscura obscura (Gmelin)   Plate 8, Fig. 6

Hawaiian names: *Amaui; Omao.* The testimony of Bloxam (1825), Andrews (1865), Dole (1879) and the very old Hawaiian whom Perkins consulted on Kauai afford evidence that the original name of the thrushes on all the islands was Amaui (Manu a Maui), and that the different island names are corruptions of this.

Dusky olive brown on upper parts, lighter on head, quills mostly dark brown, underneath ashy gray; bill black; legs and feet brown. Length 7.25 inches. It is smaller and darker than the Kauai bird. Immature birds are spotted brown and buff on the lighter plumage. There is no record of eggs or chicks.

Endemic to the island of Hawaii. It was common in September and October 1891, at about 2,000 feet elevation, not so common at 4,500 and 5,000 feet. Less common on the northern slopes of Mauna Kea and in the Kohala mountains, but it was seen wherever there was forest that the native birds still inhabited. In the bird survey of 1936-37 only one was seen. It was calling with the double note used by the Lanai species on the eastern slope of Mauna Kea. Observers since have found it not rare in the vicinity of the Hawaii National Park.

It takes short flights during which its wings make a buzzing sound, not continuous like the wing sound of the oo, but in short bursts. It sails out into the open air to catch insects and sometimes to sing a few ecstatic notes. It is a more retiring and a shyer bird than the Kauai species and also more active. Perkins found it very agile in hunting insects. He also found it migrating to parts of the forest where there was an invasion of caterpillars. Its food is largely fruit, berries, insects and caterpillars, also the fleshy flower bracts of the ieie vine. Both Perkins and Henshaw lauded its singing. Perkins noted quite a difference between its singing and that of the Kauai bird, marked by him on one occasion when he went directly from Kauai to Hawaii. He mentioned its singing early in the morning when the stars were still shining. I thought it sang less than the Kauai species.

In September and October 1891 these birds had reared their young, as numbers in the immature spotted plumage were commonly seen. But there was every sign that they were preparing to raise another brood, pairs mating, gathering leaves for nests and in specimens taken the ovaries were enlarged. One female had a well developed egg in her eggduct. Perkins found an unfinished nest in the Kona forest but was unable to investigate it further, so there is no additional information on their nesting habits.

LANAI THRUSH

Phaeornis obscura lanaiensis Wilson

Hawaiian name: Probably *Amaui*, although the present-day people of Lanai know no name for it. Wilson called it *Olomau*, which is the name of the Molokai species.

Wilson described this bird, saying: "It closely resembles *P. obscura* and *P. myadestina*, but is smaller in dimensions than either, while the bill is distinctly intermediate in size between those of the two species. The outer pair of tail-feathers alone have very slight white markings at the tip, while the abdomen and under tail-coverts are nearly pure white.

"The length of the wing from the carpal joint is only 3.65 inches, as against 4 in *P. obscura.*"

Endemic to Lanai, and now in danger of extinction. This bird was described and named by Scott B. Wilson in 1891 who included it with the Molokai species. The latter was separated from it in 1908 by Alanson Bryan. Apart from the differences enumerated by Bryan the fact that the Molokai bird is a fine singer and the Lanai species no singer at all separates them and shows their long isolation from each other.

It inhabited all the present forest, frequenting the low trees and underbrush and, unlike the other species, did not seek the highest dead trees to broadcast its few call notes which replaced the beautiful song of the other thrushes. From 1911 to 1923 this bird was under my observation as I frequently rode the bridle trails of the forest. It was at that time a common bird and its call notes could be heard constantly, especially in the north and south ends of the small Lanai forest. It declined from 1923 when the population of Lanai increased and the town of Lanai City was built. The people brought bird diseases with their poultry and these, evidently carried by mosquitoes, were fatal to the native bird population. I watched its decine till 1931. The few times I have been through the Lanai forest since 1931 the thrushes' call notes have been conspicuously absent. There is little or no hope of this bird's survival as there is of other native Lanai birds. The Lanai forest covers not more than 5,000 acres and rises to only 3,400 feet elevation. Lanai City, a town of several thousand inhabitants is within half a mile of the forest. The ancient Hawaiians did not adversely affect the native birds, but the proximity of modern populations is inimical to their well being.

The Lanai thrush is not so tame and is more retiring than the Kauai species and more often heard than seen. Its food is berries and insects.

I found a small landshell in one. It evidently nests in the thickest under-brush, probably the ieie vine or the staghorn fern. I made a special search for the nests in 1913 and though I found some which I suspected were those of this bird there was no proof of it.

MOLOKAI THRUSH

Phaeornis obscura rutha W. A. Bryan
Hawaiian names: *Amaui; Olomau.*

"Similar to *lanaiensis* but with the throat and breast much grayer; abdomen and under tail-coverts whiter; back darker olive brown; size uniformly a trifle larger; bill average longer and slightly broader."

"*Diagnostic Characters.* Uniform in color; above brown and hair-brown with an olive wash; with no conspicuous markings on outer tail feathers; size larger . . ." (Wm. Alanson Bryan "Some Birds of Molokai.") Bryan gives full descriptions. Average length taken in the flesh by Bryan 8.31 inches.

This species was included by Wilson with the Lanai species in 1891 and separated from it by Bryan in 1908. The fact that the Molokai bird is a fine singer and the Lanai species not a songster helps to justify the separation.

Endemic to Molokai, it was common in the eighteen nineties, but is now in danger of extinction. Perkins found it still inhabiting the outer forests after the other native birds had deserted the locality. Bryan collected specimens in 1907. I saw it that year but it did not seem so numerous as formerly. In the bird survey in 1936 I thought I heard one sing but was not absolutely sure. Donaghho went over a great deal of Molokai forest in 1937 but did not see it. There is a remote chance that it may survive on the elevated plateau between the Pelekunu and Wailau valleys. Increase of population on Molokai may be the cause of its disappearance as well as that of the other Molokai birds. In a month of search over miles of forest trails on Molokai in 1936 I saw but one solitary native bird. Like the Lanai thrush it frequented the low trees and did not sing so much from the highest tree tops as some of the other species.

Its feeding habits are the same as others of the genus, mostly berries and insects.

Little is known of its breeding habits. Perkins says: " . . . I found two nests of *P. lanaiensis* on the island of Molokai both fresh and apparently nearly complete. One of these was placed in an ohia tree at the height of about 25 feet from the ground in the midst of a thick forest, the other in the top of a kolea tree *(Suttonia)* at about the same height, but far below the dense forest, in a locality where no other birds except *Phaeornis* existed. In each of these cases a pair of old birds were continually in the vicinity of the nests, which were of simple structure much like those of the Drepanididae, but of much larger size, built of dried leaves, twigs, and rootlets." No eggs or chicks in the down have ever been found of which we have any record.

OAHU THRUSH

Phaeornis obscura oahuensis Wilson
Hawaiian name: *Amaui.*

Bloxam's description as given by Henshaw: "Length 7½ inches. Upper parts olive brown, extremities of the feathers much lighter color; tail and wings brown; bill bristled at the base."

This species was endemic to Oahu and inhabited its forests, but has been long extinct. It was collected and described in manuscript by Bloxam who was naturalist on the *H. M. S. Blonde* when Lord Byron brought the bodies of King Liholiho and Queen Kamamalu to Honolulu from England in 1823.

While in the islands Bloxam collected a number of specimens of Hawaiian birds and among them was the Oahu thrush. The bird became extinct, the specimens were lost, and there is no known specimen existing in the world at this time.

Bloxam and his companions spent a night on the east side of Oahu. After an uncomfortable night they made an early start up the Nuuanu pali back to Honolulu. I quote from page 43 of his diary, May 14, 1825: "We soon began to ascend the pass the sun rising at the time amid the chirping of small birds and the melodious notes of a brown thrush, the only songster on the islands." From this we learn that the species was at that time undoubtedly a common bird and like most other species of the genus was a "melodious" songster. It is a great loss to Oahu as this thrush like the Kauai and Molokai species evidently inhabited the outer fringes of the forest and the residents could fully enjoy its beautiful song.

KAUAI THRUSH

Phaeornis obscura myadestina Stejneger
Hawaiian names: *Amaui; Kamao; Kamau.*

Above dull hair-brown tinged with olive, below gray, lighter on throat and running into white on belly and under tail-coverts. Length in the flesh 9 inches. Immature birds are spotted like those of Hawaii and of other islands.

This thrush was described by Stejneger in 1887 from specimens sent to the Smithsonian Institution by Valdemar Knudsen in the eighteen eighties.

Endemic to Kauai. It was extremely common in 1891 over all the forest region of the island from near sea level on the north side and outer edges of the forest to the mountain tops. In fact it was the most common bird in the Kauai forest at that time. It was still numerous on the forest edges in 1899 when the writer left Kauai. On April 22 of that year I noted that the other birds seemed to have left the outer forest but the kamao was still there singing with great vigor. I visited the Kauai forest in September 1928, April 1931, July and August 1932, when I searched all the outside forests in vain for this bird. Only one individual was seen and it was in the depths of the forest. But in January 1936, in a visit to Kaholuamanu, at about 3,700 feet elevation, a region I had not visited since 1899, I found this bird fairly common, with others of the Kauai birds. Walter Donaghho found in 1941 that this bird was still doing well there. The elevation, remoteness from human habitation and less penetration of foreign birds has favored its survival. The Gay and Robinson family who owned a considerable amount of the forest have kept it in primeval condition and this favors the native birds. Kauai offers an exceptional opportunity for perpetuation of some of the remarkable forms of Hawaiian perching birds. If given a certain amount of care these birds might even increase again and spread over the forests at the Kokee camps to be enjoyed by numbers of people.

Its habits are much the same as the Hawaii amaui but it is much tamer. On a dead calm day I noted that the kamao would sit with wings quivering within a few feet of me, turning its head on one side with a look of mild curiosity. Its food is largely berries, like others of the genus. Like nearly all the forest birds it is fond of the fleshy flower bracts of the ieie vine. It is a beautiful singer and lavish of its song. In January, February and March, 1891 the forests resounded with its melodious notes.

At Halemanu the singing of the Phaeornis and other birds used to waken us at daybreak. It has a melancholy call and uses a hissing note at times. Like the Hawaii and Molokai birds it has the habit of rising on the wing into the air, singing a few vigorous notes and then suddenly dropping down into the underbrush. The young birds were troubled with lumps on their feet and sometimes at the corners of the mouth.

SMALL KAUAI THRUSH

Phaeornis palmeri Rothschild   Plate 8, Figs. 8 & 9
Hawaiian name: *Puaiohi.*

Adult. Upper parts dull brown, head darker, a white mark over the eye; under parts grayish, abdomen white. The type specimen was an immature male, plumage much the same in color and spotted as the young of the larger thrushes, except that it had a light mark over the eye; side feathers of its tail grayish. Its legs and bill longer and more slender in proportion than those of the larger bird. Bill black; legs flesh color. Length in the flesh with curves 7 inches.

This interesting little bird, endemic to Kauai, but very rare, no doubt originally inhabited the whole Kauai forest. Mr. F. Gay had seen it several times. He told Wilson the name *puaiohi* was better known on the northeast of Kauai and Mr. W. E. H. Deverill of Hanalei was given the name by an old native who said the bird made a hissing noise. In Palmer's first visit to the northwest side of Kauai he secured only one specimen which a rat carried off but Palmer recovered it. From this specimen Rothschild described the species and named it for the collector. Palmer returned twice in 1893 to try to get an adult but failed. Perkins made a thorough study of the species, and collected a fair number of adults, as well as immature birds. He considered it one of the rarest birds he had collected. He had seen as many as 8 in a day but rarely saw half as many. Donaghho is confident that he saw two in 1940 deep in the forest. It has not been seen in the locality where Perkins studied it, for nearly half a century.

Perkins described it as quick in its flight, flying low under the trees and difficult to follow to its destination. The type specimen was very tame. It stood high on its legs, upright on a koa branch and looked more like a flycatcher than a thrush. Perkins found it a bird of the underbrush, though it took to the high trees at times to sing. The type specimen had caterpillars and seeds in its stomach. Perkins found it largely insectivorous, feeding on beetles, spiders and caterpillars. Its special food was a beetle from the koa trees. The alarm note was a squeak, and the song a simple trill like that of the akialoa nukupuu of Hawaii. It sang from the tree tops and also on the wing like the larger thrushes. Indications in the middle of May were that the breeding season was approaching.

MAUI THRUSH

Perkins was sure that there had been a thrush on Maui as already related, but as there is no specimen or record of one ever having been seen it can be stated only as an assumption. If there ever was one it was extinct before the days of collectors on Maui.

The Miller Birds
LAYSAN MILLER BIRD

Acrocephalus familiaris Rothschild   Plate 8, Fig. 5

It was called *miller bird* because of its fondness for the large "miller" moths. Grayish brown on upper parts, wings and tail darker and underparts lighter, the little miller bird slipped about among the half dried grass almost unseen. There seemed little difference in color between the sexes or immature. Endemic to Laysan, but now extinct. It was found all over the island where there was vegetation. It hunted its food among the grass and shrubbery. It came into the laboratory through the window and hunted moths among the rafters under the roof while we worked on our specimens. At night by lamp light one hunted under the unsealed roof of Freeth's bedroom while we sat and talked. He told us of the birds breaking test tubes when the laboratory was first used for testing guano. They alighted on the edge and toppled them over. Yet they slipped about with such agility that we found them difficult to catch. But like the rail they were attracted to a pole fishnet held on the ground. They came to it looking for moths and a turn of the net trapped them.

Its food seemed to be entirely insects, moths, flies and small beetles. It swallowed large moths whole, wings and all. It had a rather nice little song, a deep harsh note a little hard; but it was the end of the breeding season and we may not have heard it at its best.

We found a number of nests. One in the top of a shrub had two eggs. It was 3 inches in diameter with a hollow in the top about 2 inches across and 1½ deep, built of grass, down and feathers. We found a number of nests with either two eggs or two chicks. The chicks had feathers budding. One swallowed a large moth with ease. One nest was lined with gooney feathers forming a fringe round the edge which nearly covered it. Eggs were bluish white with brown spots, thicker at the blunt end, .85x.65 inch. Some of the eggs instead of being spotted had a black blotch on the large end.

Rabbits devastated the vegetation of Laysan and an insectivorous bird could find no sustenance, hence its entire disappearance.

NIHOA MILLER BIRD
Acrocephalus kingi (Wetmore)

Dr. Wetmore characterized this bird as similar to the miller bird of Laysan "but throat, breast and abdomen paler, nearly white; auricular region darker; markings about eye not yellowish; upper surface much darker; bill heavier, averaging very slightly longer; tarsus heavier, slightly longer."

Endemic to Nihoa. This is one of the species missed by the Rothschild expedition through being unable to land on Nihoa. It was not discovered till 1923 when the Bishop Museum expedition landed on the island. Dr. Wetmore discovered the bird and described it, naming it for Lieut. Commander Samuel Wilder King who commanded the expedition, carried on the Minesweeper "Tanager."

The bird had remained there undisturbed for 32 years after we missed it. It is hoped that the island will remain indefinitely in its primeval condition and its flora and fauna neither added to nor diminished by the devastating hand of man. Two endemic land birds, and from 15 to 20 seabirds nest there. The difficulty in landing is effective in keeping it isolated.

The Elepaios

There is one species of the genus Chasiempis in Hawaii with three subspecies, one on each of the islands of Hawaii, Kauai and Oahu. Their ancestors are supposed to have come from the Australian side and their residence not to have been of long duration compared with the Drepanine family. All are known by the native name elepaio, though on Kauai the immature bird is known as apekepeke. The adult is a brownish bird with white markings, the immature a rufous colored bird. The latter breed and Mr. F. Gay told me he once saw a pair of apekepeke which had a nest and brown chicks in it. It is possible that the rufous bird is an aberrant form and that the young resemble it in color. The closely allied white-breasted fantail *(Rhipidura)* of New Zealand has an aberrant black form. The three species vary little in size, total length varying from 5.5 to 5.75 inches.

Why there should be no elepaio on Maui, Molokai or Lanai is not easily explained. It is possible that there had been at one time, as Alanson Bryan found evidence that it had existed on Molokai.

All the forms have habits much the same. Insect and caterpillar feeders, they catch insects on the wing and pick their other food from leaves and branches of the trees which they frequent from the topmost branches to the ground. All have a scolding note and a happy little song.

It was a sacred bird to the old Hawaiians and it was considered a bad omen if it alighted on a tree just felled for canoe building. It is a favorite with people on the islands today because it is the only Hawaiian bird that is almost unaffected by the new conditions that have decimated most of the other species of passerine birds. It is a fearless friendly bird and it is always pleasant to make its acquaintance. However, some I know of near Honolulu have lost their friendly attitude towards human beings. They can often be heard but seldom seen. The organ of the Honolulu Audubon Society is named the "Elepaio" after this bird. The elepaio's nest is the best known of the Hawaiian birds' nests. It is neat and cleverly built. Many are made of the soft scales of the tree fern, the pulu of the Hawaiians. In building, the pulu is probably held together by the bird's saliva until bound round the outside with cobweb. I have watched the bird manipulate the cobweb in its bill before placing it on the nest. So long as the web is not removed the nest holds together perfectly for many years but if the web is broken it falls to pieces at once.

Since writing the above there has come to my notice an article in the "Science News Letter" of June 19, 1943, p. 393, entitled "On-Edge Nest Holds Eggs Stuck With Natural Glue," describing the nest of the palm swift in Kenya, Africa. The information was obtained by an English ornithologist, R. E. Moreau, working in Kenya under the auspices of the Royal Society of London.

The nest is simply a pad of feathers glued together and to a "nearly vertical frond of a tall palm." The eggs are glued to a narrow ledge at the bottom of the pad. I have long suspected that the New Zealand fantail and the elepaio keep their nests from falling to pieces with glue until they bind them securely round the outside with spider's web.

KAUAI ELEPAIO

Chasiempis sandwichensis sclateri Ridgway   Plate 8, Fig. 1

Upper parts dark gray, rump and upper tail-coverts white, quills and tail feathers blackish brown, outer tail feathers tipped with white, second-, ary wing feathers with white tips; buff on throat, breast and sides of body. Length 5.59 inches. Throat and forehead of female whiter than in the male. The immature are rufous colored above and lighter below.

Endemic to Kauai, it inhabits all the forest region. It is holding well, as I found at the Kokee camps in 1936 when I set out long before daybreak to investigate a strange bird call that had been brought to my attention. I was surprised to hear the number of birds calling all over the forest before there was a sign of daylight. It was a strange call, so I stayed close to where one was calling, and as the dawn lightened the call changed gradually to the regular *weteu* of the elepaio. The call sounded so different when it was dark that the C.C.C. men encamped near the forest for over a year were puzzled with it. The call is loud for the size of the bird *weteeu* or *wituii* which often precedes a few notes of lively song.

We found several nests, one holding two eggs. The egg was about the size of an English sparrow's with reddish brown spots. One nest, which I saw being built had two tiers added to it, appearing as if a new nest had been built on top of an old one, but all were new. There was a groove around each tier which added to the deception. The nest measured six inches high and 6 in diameter. Width of depression 1.75, depth 1.5 inches. It was built up from the base of a plain prong and carried up to a leaf which hung nicely over it almost completely covering the opening of the nest, the leaf curving higher in the center. Nests were not high in the trees.

HAWAII ELEPAIO

Chasiempis sandwichensis sandwichensis (Gmelin)   Plate 8, Fig. 2

Though the Hawaii elepaio does not differ greatly from the Kauai bird my notes say it is much finer looking with more white on the wings and abdomen. The immature birds are also much the same as the young on Kauai, but their bills are darker, almost black.

This type subspecies is endemic to the island of Hawaii. Like the Kauai species it frequents all the forests and all the vegetation of the forests. Its habits are also the same: making short flights, sitting perfectly still for an instant, darting out after flying insects and searching over tree limbs and foliage, feeding on insects and caterpillars, readily attracted by an imitation of its call or any chirping sound. Its scolding notes and little song are also like those of the Kauai elepaio. Perkins describes a nest such as the three tiered one I saw on Kauai. Perkins found nests with two eggs. Henshaw saw nests with 3 eggs but as the apapane has a nest not greatly different from that of the elepaio he may have been mistaken, as the apapane lays 3 eggs.

OAHU ELEPAIO

Chasiempis sandwichensis gayi Wilson   **Plate 8, Figs. 3 & 4**

Endemic to Oahu. Described by Wilson and named after Francis Gay, it differs little in appearance or habits from the other two elepaios. It seems to me not quite so friendly to human beings as the other two. It is holding its own well in the Oahu forests from which so many of the native birds have long disappeared.

Honey Eaters

MELIPHAGIDAE   Honey-eater Family

The progenitors of the Meliphagine family in Hawaii were undoubtedly from the Australian side. The genus Acrulocercus has 4 distinct species in the Hawaiian group; one each on Hawaii, Kauai, Oahu and Molokai. They differ in appearance and habits. Some of their notes and actions remind me of the New Zealand tui (*Prosthemadera novae zealandia*) also a Meliphagine bird with which I am well acquainted.

KAUAI OO

Acrulocercus braccatus (Cassin)   **Plate 9, Fig. 4**
Hawaiian name: *Oo aa.* (Aa, a dwarf or small person; hence "the little oo.")

"*Adult male.* Head black, streaked with a few longitudinal lines of white: rest of the upper surface slaty brown, brightening into russet on the rump and flanks; throat and breast black, each feather barred with white; rest of under surface slaty brown, while the centers of the feathers being grey give it a streaked appearance; wings and tail black, the central pair of feathers of the latter much exceeding the rest in length; axillary tufts (little developed) of a pale greyish buff; edge of the wing pure white; tibiae rich golden yellow; irides light yellow; bill and feet black."

"*Adult female.* Similar to the male, but with the feathers of the throat much more extensively barred with white, which gives the bird the appearance of having a well defined whitish patch on the throat and upper part of the breast." (Wilson.) Length about 7.75 inches.

An immature bird shot in May 1891 had under parts lighter than the adult; wings and tail glossy black; yellow on legs and white on wings absent; bill and legs lighter than those of the adult; loose skin at base of beak white; iris bluish grey. Some older were in duller plumage than the adults. (From my notes in May 1891.) There is no record of eggs or chicks.

Endemic to Kauai and now in danger of extinction. In 1891 it was a common bird over all the Kauai forests. Its notes could be heard from near sea-level in the valleys on the north side to near the top of Mt. Waialeale at over 4,000 feet elevation. It was still not uncommon when I left Kauai in 1899, but on four visits to the Kauai forests between 1928 and 1936 I failed to hear or see it. In 1936 I thought I heard one sing but could not be sure. Had it given its call note I could easily have identified it. Donaghho penetrated deep into the Kauai forest in 1940 and is sure that he heard it. He had no previous experience with the Hawaiian oos so may have been mistaken. However, if it still exists no effort should be spared to save what would be the last of the famous Hawaiian oos.

An active bird, quick in movements in hunting food, quick in flight when darting through the trees, but not often flying high above the tree tops like the Hawaii oo. It was the most noisy and most entertaining bird in the Kauai forest both in song and action. When hunting its food in the dry loose bark clinging to the ohia branches its presence was often betrayed by the rustling noise it made. Hopping along the branches with its tail erect over its back or hanging sideways on the trunk with its strong claws and braced with its stiff tail, with a wild keen look in its grayish yellow eyes it was a picture of energy and alertness.

Cockroaches, spiders, millipeds, crickets and other insects and caterpillars taken mostly from under the loose bark were its principal food. The fleshy flower bracts of the ieie vine is also in its dietary, as is honey from the flowering ohia and other trees.

The call note was a distinct *took took* like the Hawaii species but sharper and higher pitched. Its distress cry was a scream like that made by a wounded New Zealand tui. As a singer it was among the finest of the native Hawaiian birds. Both male and female sang, the latter with fewer notes. In March and April there were all the signs that this species was laying or hatching. A nest out of reach in a kukui tree likely belonged to an oo. It appeared to be built of small twigs and grass and was about 5 inches in diameter. It also had the appearance of the nest of the tui. Perkins described similar nests which he judged to be of this bird. In May Mr. Gay and I collected some young birds.

The yellow feathers on the leg were used by the Hawaiians in their feather work. They were smaller and not nearly so fine as the plumes of the other oos and their gathering was early discontinued.

MOLOKAI OO

Acrulocercus bishopi Rothschild
Other name: *Bishop's Oo.*

"*Adult male.* Head and occiput deep black with a very slight metallic gloss, the shafts of the feathers a little paler. Neck, back, breast and abdomen smoky black, with narrow white shaft lines to the feathers. Rump and upper tail-coverts black. Wings and wing-coverts black. Tail black with very narrow white fringes to the tip. The two middle tail feathers long and pointed, ear-coverts with an elongated tuft of golden yellow feathers, these feathers black at lowest base. Axillary tufts bright yellow, shorter than in *Moho nobilis.* Under tail-coverts bright yellow. Iris dark brown. Bill and feet black; soles dark flesh color with a yellow tinge. Total length 11 to 11.75 inches. The female is similar in color to the male, but smaller." (Rothschild.)

Endemic to Molokai and in danger of extinction, Bishop's oo was discovered by Palmer in 1892 at Kaluaaha, Molokai. Rothschild named it after Mr. Charles R. Bishop who founded the Bishop Museum. It frequented the upper forest of Molokai. Perkins was able to make a good study of it. He found that the natives used to snare it for its yellow plumes. An old native woman showed him a number of these feathers, some loose and some tied in bundles with olona fiber. He traced marks of the bird lime with which the birds were snared, on the feathers. Members of the Meyer family collected a number of these birds in the 1880's and have some still in their possession. I saw a group of about half a dozen in 1904, the last authentic instance of its being seen. A mutilated specimen of one of these is in the Bishop Museum. Alanson Bryan and I both failed to find it in 1907. I was informed that it frequented the Wailau trail in 1915 but there is no certainty of this. On the bird survey in 1936 I failed to find it and Donaghho has been over a great deal of Molokai trails with the same result. It may still exist on the plateau between the Pelekunu and Wailau gulches.

The group I saw were active birds in the low trees on the gulch wall. They were inquisitive and though they approached me closely, they were timid and continually on the alert, never still an instant, chattering continuously. They stayed for some time before taking fright and leaving.

Its food was largely nectar, preferring honey from the lobelia flowers and even confining itself to certain species of those wonderful plants, according to Perkins. It also took insects. It had a loud seasonal call, "*owow, owow-ow*," audible at a distance of 3,000 feet. Nothing is known of its nest, eggs or young.

HAWAII OO

Acrulocercus nobilis (Merrem)   Plate 9, Fig. 5

"*Adult male.* General color black inclining to dull umber on the abdomen, axillary tufts bright yellow; terminal half of the two outer pairs of tail-quills white; middle pair of tail-quills greatly elongated and spirally twisted; irides dark hazel; bill and feet black. Total length 12.5 inches."

"*Adult female.* Similar in color to the male, but with middle pair of tail feathers not nearly so much elongated or twisted. Total length 9.5 inches." (Wilson.) Immature birds lack the yellow axillary tufts.

Endemic to the island of Hawaii, evidently at one time inhabiting all its forests, but now in danger of extinction. In 1891 and '92 it was common above Kawaaloa in Kona but by 1894 it had disappeared from there. The influx of coffee farmers with their fowls and bird diseases no doubt wiped out this beautiful bird. Henshaw stated that numbers were shot for their plumes and no doubt this helped to destroy it. It survived longer in some other places. In the bird survey 1936-37 the only trace I could find of it was one that had been heard on the slopes of Mauna Loa near the Hawaii National Park about 1934 but had disappeared.

A small lot of 3 males and 2 females were received alive by the Gay and Robinson family in 1892 and released at Makaweli, Kauai. They survived for a time but eventually disappeared.

Above Kawaloa they were very active hopping about in the tree tops in the early morning and evening, often in small companies, and quieter in the heat of the day unless the air was cooled with light showers. Their flight is not rapid. Their wings move quickly with a continuous buzzing, a sound different than that made by other forest birds. They do not have the agility of the Kauai oo in darting through the foliage and undergrowth. In flight they keep above the trees perhaps on account of the long unwieldy tail. These birds are very shy, flying off as soon as a human being is sighted. Even the breaking of a twig startles them. We found it difficult to see them when they were sitting quietly in the tree tops. Their food is principally nectar from the ohia flowers and arborescent lobelias; insects and caterpillars are also taken. At the time we collected in Kona they were feeding almost exclusively on the flower bracts of the ieie as were nearly all the birds of the vicinity. Several oos were seen feeding on it and one was shot when so engaged. Their stomachs contained little else.

Their voice is a deep '*took took*' with which they answered each other continuously when active. Both males and females have a few notes of song. When singing they seem to have difficulty in producing the notes, ruffling the feathers and jerking the body in their effort. The song of the Hawaii oo is not so loud, vigorous or pleasing as that of the Kauai species. We found it difficult to trace the bird from its call notes. It seemed to be closer than it really was. Henshaw also noticed this. Perkins found it breeding above Kawaloa in September, and caught young birds recently from the nest. There is no record of nests or eggs having been examined.

The beautiful bright yellow axillary plumes were prized for the wonderful feather work of the Hawaiians. The birds were probably snared for this. Whether they were released or killed and eaten is not known. The latter was probably the case. This, however, would not take even the natural increase. Simple as it might have been to snare some kinds of birds, to snare the oo must have been difficult. I saw at Waimea, Kauai in 1891 a kahili made from the central tail quills of the Hawaii oo.

OAHU OO

Acrulocercus apicalis Gould   Plate 9, Fig. 3

Description (from Gould): "General plumage sooty black; tail brown, all but the two middle feathers largely tipped with white; the two central feathers somewhat narrower than the others, and gradually diminishing in the apical third of their length into fine hairlike or filamentous upturned points; axillae or under surface of the shoulder white; flanks and under tail-coverts bright yellow: bill and legs black. Total length 12 inches, bill 1½, wing 4, tail 6, tarsi 1½ inches.

"The plumage of the female is in every respect similar to that of the male; but, as in the honey-eaters of Australia generally; . . . the body is fully a fourth less in size . . ." (Wilson.)

Endemic to Oahu and probably extinct. According to Scott.B. Wilson in his "Birds of the Sandwich Islands," there are only 5 specimens of the Oahu oo in museums, two in Germany and three in Great Britain. Two were collected by Captain Dixon in 1787, one by Byron in 1826 and two by Deppe in 1837. According to Sanford B. Dole in his "Synopsis of the Hawaiian Birds," its native name and habits were the same as the Hawaii species. I did not collect on Oahu in the 1890's but Perkins who worked the Oahu forests very thoroughly said that this bird "was almost certainly extinct." If the Oahu oo had as loud a call as those of Hawaii, Kauai and Molokai it would soon betray its presence to anyone traversing the forest to any extent.

KIOEA

Chaetoptila angustipluma (Peale)   Plate 9, Fig. 1

The word *kioea* means to stand high, as on long legs. The name is descriptive of both the birds which bear it, this one and the curlew.

The upper parts of this bird are mostly brown and the underparts dull white, but it has a variety of markings which are shown in the colored plate. Length 13 inches.

Endemic to the island of Hawaii, but long extinct. Pickering and Peale of the United States Exploring Expedition in 1840 collected one specimen of this bird. They found it frequenting the tall flowering trees. Mills collected several specimens about 1859. Dole gave the name kioea for it, and said it inhabited Hawaii and Molokai. The curlew, also called kioea, was then common on Molokai and Dole was probably mistaken in assigning *Chaetoptila* to that island. There are points of general resemblance between the two birds, such as standing high on their legs which may have caused the natives to call them by the same name. Collectors in the eighteen-nineties found no trace of it. Perkins was of the opinion that *Chaetoptila* arrived on these islands from the Australian side much later than the oo.

Pickering and Peale described it as a lively bird. It was a honeysucker and like the other Hawaiian honeyeaters no doubt also fed on insects and caterpillars. Peale described its call as a loud *chuck* and said also that it was something of a singer. Nothing is known of its nest, eggs, or young.

Hawaiian Honey-creepers

DREPANIDIDAE   Hawaiian Honey-creeper Family

There was considerable confusion in the classification of the birds now recognized as belonging to this family. Some were classed as finches, others as honeyeaters. Through the investigations (1892-1902) of Dr. R. C. L. Perkins it was eventually made clear that both the thick-billed species and the long thin-billed and intermediate forms were all descended from one or possibly two honeyeating ancestral species.

Authorities are agreed that most likely the ancestors of this family came originally from the American side. To all appearances they came very early before other land birds, probably when vegetation was plentiful. No enemies and a plentiful food supply permitted a large increase and caused keen competition among themselves. This competition through ages caused recourse to other sources of food supply and eventual physical adaptation so as to permit easy access to these sources. To enumerate some of the extreme forms: *Hemignathus* with long beaks and long tongues to extract honey from the deep tubular flowers that prevailed in the early life of these islands, and to capture grubs and beetles from holes and crevices in bark and wood; *Pseudonestor*, with a parrot-like bill capable of splitting the hard twigs of the koa *(Acacia koa)* and extracting hidden grubs; *Chloridops* with a massive bill and strong jaw-muscles to break the hard dry seeds of the naio *(Myoporum)*. It is on the minute seed germ which this little nut contains that this bird feeds almost exclusively. *Rhodacanthis* with a strong sharp-edged bill to cut up the large green beans and seed pods of the koa, and large stomach to hold this massive food; *Psittacirostra* with a hooked bill to scoop out the ripe ieie fruit *(Freycinetia)* from its upright stem; *Loxoides* with a hooked bill suitable for opening the beans of the mamane *(Sophora)*. Such birds as *Pseudonestor* and *Chloridops* had an inexhaustable food supply inaccessible to other birds of the Hawaiian forests, or even of birds closely allied to them.

There are 17 genera and 43 species and subspecies listed in the Drepanine family, which Perkins has divided into two groups, the Melano-drepanine group comprising those genera which are basically black or

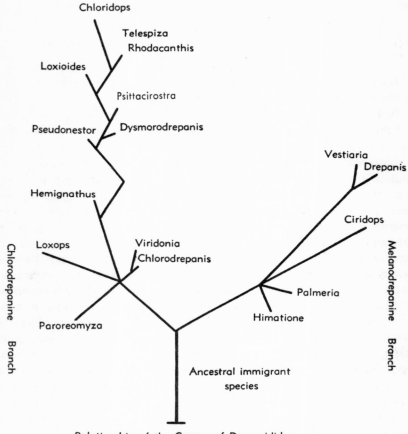

Chloridops

Telespiza
Rhodacanthis

Loxioides

Psittacirostra

Pseudonestor   Dysmorodrepanis

Vestiaria
Drepanis

Hemignathus

Ciridops

Loxops   Viridonia
Chlorodrepanis

Palmeria

Paroreomyza   Himatione

Chlorodrepanine   Branch

Melanodrepanine   Branch

Ancestral immigrant
species

Relationship of the Genera of Drepanididae
After Dr. R. C. L. Perkins

which have an appreciable admixture of black in their plumage, and the Chlorodrepanine group, comprising the genera which are basically yellow or green, or at least completely lacking black. This matter of coloration is not the only distinction between the groups, but it is the most conspicuous. The five genera of the Melanodrepanine branch are discussed first.

MAMO

Drepanis pacifica (Gmelin)   Plate 10, Fig. 9

Cook's naturalists referred to the *Mamo* as *Hoohoo*, probably confusing it with the *Oo*, also a black bird with some yellow feathers.

Rothschild describes the adult male that Palmer obtained as "Black with a slight gloss. Rump and upper tail-coverts, the shoulders, the ridge of the wing, the outer part of the under wing-coverts, thighs and under tail-coverts all of a beautiful rich yellow, but paler on the ridges of the wing . . ." Then he goes on with details of description and gives "Total length in the flesh as 9.375, in the skin 8 inches." (Measurements of lengths are explained in the Preface.)

Endemic to the island of Hawaii. This remarkable bird is probably now extinct. It likely inhabited all the Hawaii forests, since it is known to have occurred in both the leeward and windward forests as well as in the Kohala mountains. Mills collected some about 1859. It was not an extremely rare bird up to the eighteen-eighties. Perkins had a record that in 1880 one man bagged with a shotgun as many as 12 in one day. It was then being shot for its feathers. Perkins was of the opinion that in the 1890's specimens of this bird might have been obtained under favorable circumstances.

Palmer secured one specimen in 1892, the only one taken since Mills secured his and none have been taken since. Henshaw saw a small group in 1899. He described their flight as "Not rapid, but was smooth and well sustained." It reminded him of the cuckoo in flight. Palmer's specimen as recorded by Wolstenholme was apparently quite tame. He said it roosted on a stick in the tent. He gave me a photo of it perched on his finger. This bird was taken deep in the Olaa forest where Wolstenholme and the Hawaiians were in camp. The old bird catcher Ahulu recognized the call of the bird across a valley. His imitation of the call brought the bird. He set a snare by the flower of a haha *(Clermontia)* growing on the trunk of a tree fern. Ahulu called the bird to the snare and caught it.

The mamo was a nectar feeding bird, but whether it ate insects also is not known. The captive bird sucked sugar and water eagerly. The old bird catchers gave Perkins an exhibition of its call, a single rather long and plaintive note. It was so like the call of the nearly related Molokai mamo, with which he was well acquainted that he had no doubt of its correctness.

The mamo is famed for having furnished the most beautiful feathers for the Hawaiian feather work. The birds were caught with birdlime and also with the noose. A bird so tame and coming readily to call could easily be caught by the simple method the native boys on Kauai used in supplying the naturalist Townsend (1835) with specimens. Hidden by bushes bearing tubular flowers the boy held up a flower between finger and thumb and as the honeyeating bird dipped its bill into it he closed his finger on the flower and captured the bird by the bill. It is not known whether the birds were killed or released after the choice feathers were removed. The inference is that they were killed and eaten. The Hawaiians were eager for meat and the birds, if denuded of the yellow feathers covering so much of their bodies would surely succumb, especially in the wet and cold upper forests. But with the mamo as with the oo, the natural increase must have been very great when the forests were in their natural state and before changed conditions had reduced the numbers of the birds. The yearly take of birds at that time would, I think, have been little drain on their numbers. Introduced diseases and the shotgun brought the changed conditions which probably account for their extinction.

Nothing is known of the breeding habits of the mamo.

PERKINS' MAMO

Drepanis funerea Newton   Plate 10, Fig. 8

Hawaiian names: *Oo-nuku-umu; Hoa.* The first name, recorded by Perkins, means "the oo with the sucking beak." The other name was recorded much later by W. A. Bryan.

Discovered in 1893 by Perkins, who obtained the name from an old native woman in Pelekunu valley. She knew of the birds and showed him yellow feathers from the Molokai oo. From its dark color the natives would naturally consider it a species of oo.

Lusterless black, white on quill feathers, bill long and curved, upper mandible longer than lower, legs and beak black, beak longer in the male. Length about 8 inches.

Endemic to Molokai and in danger of extinction. Perkins collected a series of skins, and private collectors later depleted the district above Pelekunu valley where Perkins had collected. Neither Alanson Bryan nor I could find any there in 1907, but Bryan secured 3 male specimens at Moanui farther round the island to the east. The survey in 1936 found only a rumor that one had been seen in the Wailau valley a few years before. Donaghho traversed much of the Molokai forest in 1937 and found no trace of it. But even the common birds were gone then. Possibly it may still exist on the plateau between Wailau and Pelekunu valleys. This plateau is the only hope of refuge for survival of the Molokai native forest birds.

It was a bird of the underbrush and low forest trees. Its food was mostly honey from certain arborescent species of lobelioids. Perkins thought that it alone sufficed to fertilize these lobelias. Botanists have since disagreed with this. However, his specimens, and Bryan's also, had their heads smeared with the pollen of this flower. Perkins found no insect remains in their stomachs. One, probing into wet moss, was evidently after water as when examined it had no signs of insects in it. The young may be fed on caterpillars and insects but of this there is no proof.

It was very inquisitive and approached closely, following the intruder, making it more difficult to collect good specimens than if it kept to a distance.

Perkins said it had a loud cry of extraordinary clearness and also a milder call note which he likened to the call of the mamo. This Bryan described as *hoa* and said also that the natives gave him hoa as the name of the bird.

Perkins considered it one of the rarest birds he collected, and he made a thorough study of it. He saw as many as 7 in one day, when not equipped for bird collecting, yet he might go for several days searching for it and not see one.

IIWI

Vestiaria coccinea (Forster)   Plate 10, Figs. 1 & 2
Other Hawaiian names: *Iwi; Iawi; Iiwipolena* or *Ahikipolena* or shortened to *Polena; Olokele* (Kauai). A greenish-yellow form, the young black-spotted, is known as *Iiwipopolo*.

With bright scarlet body, black wings and tail, and rose colored, inch long, curved bill, the iiwi is one of the most beautiful of the Hawaiian native birds. Its length is about 5.75 inches. I quote from my journal in February and March 1891, at Kaholuamanu, Kauai: "The iiwi and apapane are so numerous that in their ceaseless activity, flying backwards and forwards their wings keep up a continual buzz. There will be half a dozen in a tree at a time, flitting from flower to flower and hopping about among the twigs and leaves in search of caterpillars. The iiwi also frequents the small *Pelea* trees whose flowers are borne on the trunks and branches where the birds, then very tame, can be watched from a few feet. The forest would be very monotonous were it not for these beautiful birds darting about, chasing one another, and running nimbly along the branches. Their scarlet bodies and black wings show up to great advantage. The apapane are about as plentiful but keep more to the tree tops." It seemed to me that the ohia honey had a stimulating effect as these birds were full of life and gaiety when frequenting the profusely blooming ohia trees.

Endemic to the main group they spread over all the forested islands from the mountain tops to the seashore wherever forests reached. It flew high in the air and frequented the flowering tree tops, dropping down to sip from the lower nectar bearing trees and shrubs. In high winds numbers were blown down to the lowlands and died there. Originally when the islands were forested to the seashore, they could work their way back. They followed the flowering of the ohia trees at the different elevations and gathered in great numbers at these places. Originally extremely numerous it is now greatly reduced. In 1923 it was fairly common on Lanai but diminished year by year till, by 1929, it had disappeared entirely. In the survey (1935-37) it was found on Kauai, Hawaii and Maui but none were seen on Molokai or Lanai. It will hold out perhaps indefinitely, in the larger and higher forests but only on Kauai is there a possibility of its increasing to the former spectacular numbers. If some protection from introduced diseases is afforded the Kauai native forest birds, I believe this can be accomplished.

The iiwi is very fond of nectar from flowers but feeds largely on caterpillars. It has a number of calls; a sharp chirp when feeding and a longer call note. It may have different songs, Perkins calls the song harsh, strained and discordant. My journal says, when I heard it first in January 1891, "like the creaking of a wheelbarrow but a little more musical." Henshaw says: "The disconnected notes of its rather sweet song may be heard coming all day from the tall ohias when in blossom." Both Perkins and I noticed that in a great assembly of birds the medley of sounds produced by hundreds of apapane, iiwi and other birds produced a pleasing chorus and cheerful effect. When singing in the low trees where it can be viewed closely, it seems to have difficulty in producing its notes judging by the contortions of its neck and body, and its notes then are certainly harsh and discordant.

Perkins describes the nest as of neither a compact or neat appearance, built of dry stems, leaves and rootlets and some of the skeletonized capsules of the poha, generally in tall ohia trees.

The iiwi furnished feathers for the Hawaiian feather work. The bird was caught by the various devices used for the mamo: birdlime, snares and other means.

CRESTED HONEYEATER

Palmeria dolei (Wilson)　　　　　　　　　　Plate 10, Fig. 7
Hawaiian name: *Akohekohe.*

The colored plate shows the variety of colors and the odd crest on the forehead and occiput of this remarkable bird. Length about 7 inches.

Discovered by Wilson in the late 1880's, but he secured only a very young specimen on Maui. Palmer collected adults and from these Rothschild established the genus *Palmeria*. Wilson had previously described the bird as *Himatione dolei* after Judge Sanford Ballard Dole, later President of the Hawaiian Provisional Government. The name thus becomes *Palmeria dolei*. Dole's "Synopsis of the Birds of the Hawaiian Islands" was the only publication on the Hawaiian birds available when we arrived in Honolulu in December 1890. Perkins studied this species on Maui and Molokai. I never saw the bird in life. Alanson Bryan collecting on Molokai in 1907 saw a small group on the wing but did not secure a specimen. It has not been seen since. The only hope for it on Molokai is that some may be on the plateau already mentioned or in the higher and deeper forests of Maui.

Perkins found it localized in habitat but abundant where it did occur. He thought that it, as well as other birds, abandoned regions which cattle had invaded, but it was gone from parts of the Molokai forest long before cattle penetrated it. In fact large areas of forest on Molokai have never been entered by cattle and the birds are practically all gone. In 1936 I tramped many miles of new boggy but passable trails through forest where cattle had never entered and saw no signs of native birds.

Perkins describes its habits as being like those of the apapane. Its food was largely nectar from the ohia blossoms, though it also fed on caterpillars. When feeding on honey it, like the other honey eating birds, was very aggressive towards the smaller honeysucking species and repeatedly drove them from the tree. It responded readily to an imitation of its call, a simple clear whistle, and Perkins records calling as many as 9 adult birds into one tree. He says its song is different from that of all the other birds but has notes resembling some of those of both the iiwi and apapane, and says: "Its song like that of the iiwi appears to be forced out with difficulty and lacks all beauty."

They appeared to be preparing to nest in February and March. Nothing is known of the nest or eggs.

APAPANE

Himatione sanguinea (Gmelin)   Plate 10, Figs. 5 & 6
Other Hawaiian names: *Akapane; Akakani.*

Akakane was the name given us for the Loxops of Hawaii.

Length about 5.25 inches. Body crimson, wings and tail black, as also bill and legs. Belly and under tail-coverts white; this feature serving to distinguish it from the iiwi when flying overhead. The iiwi has no white on the under parts of its body. First plumage is brown which gradually changes to the adult crimson color. Small chicks have pink skins and bunches of fluffy brownish down on their backs; as they get older the light pink skins become almost red.

Endemic to the main group where it inhabited all the forested islands from the highest level of forest to its lowest. It was extremely numerous, and often was carried by high winds to the lowlands and sometimes even to Niihau. At one time a group was evidently carried to Laysan Island where it became modified and formed a new species. The bird survey (1935-37) found it in fair numbers on Hawaii, Maui, Oahu and Kauai, a few on Lanai and but one seen on Molokai, the only native bird seen on the island at that time.

It is a strong flier, vibrating its wings loudly in flight. It flies in small companies high in the air from one part of the forest to another. The birds are very active in the tree tops, hopping from flower to flower sipping honey and stopping but a few seconds at each, or hunting through the foliage after insects and caterpillars which, with nectar, form its principal food.

Plate 11

1. *Oahu Amakihi*
2. *Anianiau*
3. *Oahu Amakihi—Male*
4. *Kauai Amakihi*
5. *Hawaii Amakihi*
6. *Ula-ai-hawane*

It has several calls and a sprightly song not particularly musical but cheerful; however, in continuous repetition by one bird it becomes monotonous. When large numbers are calling and singing together with other birds the effect is pleasing.

On Lanai in 1913-14 I made a special study of a number of nests of this bird. They were cleverly placed so as to be hidden from above as a protection from owls which are numerous and hunt over the open country contiguous to the forest and which sometimes hunt over the tree tops. The nests are generally built in the scrubby ohia trees *(Metrosideros)* 7 to 10 feet from the ground. They are about 4 by 6 inches in size, the bowl at the top 2 inches across and 2 deep. The material on the outside is a layer of grass, moss or twigs and a layer of pulu (soft down from the tree fern) and generally lined with fine grass. The nests are soft and not at all compact. Several had 3 eggs or 3 chicks and one had young nearly fledged. The birds deserted one nest, perhaps because I bent a twig over it the better to protect it, and the chicks died. Despite the careful protection by the birds several were robbed, apparently by owls, as the bottoms of the nests were pulled up showing the chicks had held on to them. Eggs, three in a clutch .69x.5 inch, white with streaky reddish brown spots thicker in a band round the large end. The feathers of the apapane were used to some extent in the Hawaiian feather work but were not especially favored as they did not show well at a distance.

There is every prospect that this bird will continue to survive but will not likely attain the numbers of the past unless in some of the most favorable forests.

LAYSAN HONEYEATER

Himatione freethi Rothschild   Plate 10, Figs. 3 & 4

Adult about the size and shape of an apapane but the color of the body duller, wings and tail brown. Iris brown; bill and legs black. Immature light brownish color.

There seems to be some confusion concerning the correct spelling of the specific name of the bird. Rothschild very evidently intended to name it in honor of Captain Freeth, but in his original description, published in 1892, he misspelled the name, in its latinized form, as *fraithii*. In publishing the "Avifauna of Laysan" in 1893, the spelling was altered in the text to the correct form, *freethi*, although the original spelling was retained on the plate, which was apparently printed before the text. The amended form of the name was followed by Wilson (1899) and Perkins (1903), but Henshaw (1902) kept the original form. Bryan's list (1942) used the spelling *fraithi.* I employ here the form intended by the author of the name.

Endemic to the island of Laysan; it frequented the grass tops, portulaca and other plants fringing the lagoon. It was not so common as the other land birds, yet not scarce. It is now quite extinct. The last three were seen by Wetmore when he arrived on the island in 1923. They disappeared in a sand storm which lasted for 3 days after his arrival. The island, formerly nearly all covered with vegetation, had been rendered a sandy desert by rabbits.

It was not so fearless and tame as the other birds but could be caught with a handnet. It was a weak, low flier. A number gathered round a small isolated house where barrels caught rain water from the roof. The birds drank from leaks in the barrels. They seemed to miss water more than the other land birds. Perhaps their residence on the island was not so long as that of the other birds, and they had not become adapted to the meager supply of water. The only natural water on the island was a seep of brackish water where the land birds may have been able to obtain a little moisture. There were of course occasional showers and there may at times have been a little dew. In the case of heavy rains large areas of the interior were under water as related by Dr. A. M. Bailey in the "Audubon Magazine" May-June 1942.

Its food was insects, caterpillars and honey from flowers. Like the other insect eating birds it liked the large "miller" moths. When eating them it held them in its claw (Freeth said always the left claw). One I watched picked away the body of the moth a bit at a time rejecting the wings and other hard parts. We saw it visiting the flowers of the Nohu *(Tribulus)* and Pohuehue *(Ipomoea)* and probably other morning glories. It had a sweet little song of a few notes. We found no nests. The wrecking of Laysan Island with the loss of its interesting land birds is one of the most deplorable examples of failure to protect to come under my observation. It is hoped that when Laysan recovers and war clouds disappear it will be given the care it deserves; but two of its interesting little birds are gone forever. The rich potentialities of Laysan, if given a chance to develop would make it a show place.

ULA-AI-HAWANE

Ciridops anna (Dole)   Plate 11, Fig. 6

The name means the red bird that feeds on the hawane (the native Hawaiian palm, *Pritchardia spp.*)

Total length about 4.25 inches. The black crown and gray neck of this bird is a striking feature, and a glimpse of a bird's head and neck showing this characteristic color made me almost sure I saw one in 1937. That was on the Kahua ditch trail which passes through the region where the Hawaiian procured the specimen for Palmer. It seems unlikely that I saw this bird but it is possible.

Endemic to the island of Hawaii. Extremely rare and perhaps extinct. According to Perkins it was known to have inhabited both the Kona and Hilo districts as well as the Kohala mountains. He quotes Emerson to the effect that it was "wild and shy, a great fighter, a bird very rarely taken by the hunter." Specimens were taken by Mills about 1859. Dole described the species from these and mistaking it for a finch called it *Fringilla anna.* It has since been found to be a drepanid and its generic name changed to *Ciridops* but it still retains the specific name Dole gave it. As indicated by its Hawaiian name the bird was reputed to feed on the fruit of the hawane palm *(Pritchardia).*

We were fortunate in obtaining one specimen of this bird but were disappointed in not securing more. We had information that the ula-ai-hawane and the mamo at one time frequented the interior of the forest of the Kohala mountains. We cut our way through the primeval wet forest to a considerable depth but failed to find any but the common birds. On leaving Kohala Palmer offered a reward for specimens of these birds. Enterprising natives penetrated deeper into the forest and secured an immature ula-ai-hawane. They reported that there were more in the locality where the specimen was obtained. Palmer then organized a party of five and we spent an arduous week penetrating the boggy mountain top till from the tree tops we could see Mauna Kea and part of the Waimea plains. We judged we had topped the watershed as the streams ran in two directions, one towards Waipio and the other towards Kohala.

We shot an akepa *(Loxops)* and then found that the natives had confused this bird with the ula-ai-hawane, hence had given the information that there were more of the latter there. There were plenty of akepa to be found but none of the bird we wanted. We searched through groves of its food plant, the hawane palm but without success, although there were flowers as well as fruit on these trees, and we shot an amakihi when it was visiting the flowers. The weather broke and we were compelled to relinquish our hunt. Palmer offered a reward for more specimens but with no results.

The Amakihis

"With [the genus] *Chlorodrepanis* we pass to the second series of genera which may be called *Chlorodrepanine* as opposed to the *Melanodrepanine* section, the latter containing all those genera which have previously been dealt with." (Perkins.)

Perkins was of the opinion that there were only three well marked species of this genus, two on Kauai and one inhabiting Hawaii, Molokai, Maui, Oahu and Lanai. I have great faith in Perkins' conclusions as he made a long study of the Hawaiian birds in their natural haunts, dissected them, made specimens of them and studied prepared specimens of them in the museums. He studied them with the keen perception of an entomologist who has to consider minute points in the structure of his specimens. This wide experience gave him a marked advantage over all others in the study of Hawaiian birds. No one ever did or ever can study the Hawaiian birds as did Dr. R. C. L. Perkins. As one of his closest friends here in Hawaii I know well the thoroughness of his investigations.

The various species of *Chlorodrepanis* carry the odor that it is a distinctive feature in so many of this family, to a degree greater than most of the others.

The different species of Chlorodrepanis differ little in size, their total length varying from 4.2 to 4.75 inches. *C. parva* is the smallest.

KAUAI AMAKIHI

Chlorodrepanis virens stejnegeri (Wilson)   Plate 11, Fig. 4
Other Hawaiian name: *Aalawi* (*Kihikihi*, or simply *kihi*, means *curved*, and refers to the curved bill of the bird. The word is used in the names of several birds with curved bills.)

Its bright green upper parts, yellowish under parts and heavier bill distinguish it from the other small birds of the Kauai forest. I noted particularly in skinning that the muscles on the back of its head were more strongly developed than in the other Kauai birds and its skull more heavily built. This development was evidently occasioned by its habit of digging in the bark of trees to a greater extent than any of the other Kauai birds; or other amakihis. Total length 4.6 inches.

Endemic to Kauai. In 1891 it occurred in great numbers inhabiting all of the Kauai forest. Its numbers have been considerably diminished but is still one of the most common birds of that island. There is every prospect of it continuing indefinitely.

It is strong on the wing and on its feet. I was surprised at the way it could dash into a bush and alight without slackening speed at all. When feeding in the ohia flowers its action is different from that of the iiwi and apapane which pass over the flowers quickly. The amakihi is much more leisurely in its movements when feeding. It probes in the crevices of the bark and hunts in the folds of leaves. It will persevere for a considerable time in obtaining something from a folded leaf, a chrysalis or spider's egg-sac. It even dug into rotten wood somewhat as does the akialoa nukupuu of Hawaii.

Insects, grubs, caterpillars, honey from flowers, berries and fruit, all form its dietary. On January 29, 1891, they and other birds were very numerous on the koa flowers. There is little or no honey in the koa blossoms so they were either getting insects or eating the plentiful pollen.

It has a distinctive call note *tseet* which it repeats at intervals when feeding or on the wing. During the mating season they sing a little song.

The laying season is about March. They were singing at that time and one specimen had a well developed egg in its egg channel. We did not find nests then nor did I at any later period.

HAWAII AMAKIHI

Chlorodrepanis virens virens (Gmelin)   Plate 11, Fig. 5

The adult of this bird seemed to me to be much more yellow than the Kauai species, and had a smaller bill. The young birds in duller plumage are difficult to tell from the young of the Hawaii creeper (*Paroreomyza*) and we, who had collected only on Kauai, at first sometimes confused both, while alive, with the young of *C. parva*. *C. parva* is now known to be restricted to Kauai, but the birds of Hawaii were quite unknown to us at that time, and there was little literature to guide us.

Endemic to the Island of Hawaii. It was numerous in all its forests, but I doubt if it is now as numerous as the amakihi of Kauai. I noted its habits, like those of the Kauai species, of stopping suddenly in full flight, of searching dead leaves for food and of visiting a great variety of flowers. I think this search is more for insects attracted by honey or pollen than for honey alone. The time taken over each flower is needless for honey only. I saw it going from flower to flower of the ieie. It was evidently after insects as the male stems of the ieie are laden with pollen and no doubt attracted some favorite insect. If feeding on the flower bracts it could easily satisfy itself in one visit. As its bill is too short to reach the bottom of the tubular flowers of the lobelias it pierces them at the bottom to obtain honey or insects.

There were many immature birds in Kona in September. Their habit of searching dead leaves for food made it difficult to tell when they were gathering leaves for a nest.

MAUI AMAKIHI
Chlorodrepanis virens wilsoni Rothschild

Endemic to Maui. I did not collect on Maui till February 1928. In the forest at Olinda it was fairly common at that time and I collected some specimens for the Bishop Museum under special permit.

Its habits did not differ from the amakihi of the other islands so far as I could see. Perkins notes of it that "the amakihi here when at its best often sings much more loudly than at other times."

MOLOKAI AMAKIHI
Chlorodrepanis virens kalaana

Endemic òn Molokai, but differing little, if at all, from the species of Maui, Lanai and Oahu.

LANAI AMAKIHI
Chlorodrepanis virens chloroides (Wilson)

Endemic to Lanai. This bird was very common in the Lanai forest and was still there a few years ago but very much reduced in numbers since the pineapple plantation was started with its large influx of population. Its chances of survival are slight as is true of all the Lanai native forest birds. The only explanation for this is the introduction of new bird diseases. I lived on Lanai for 20 years and saw the birds increasing, if anything, till 1923 when the town was built. With the speedy increase of population and greater numbers of domestic fowls the birds began to decrease perceptibly. The native forest is small, of no considerable elevation, and in close proximity to the settlement, offering no protection through isolation. These same conditions pertain to Molokai in slightly different degrees.

I saw only one nest of the amakihi on Lanai. That was on April 13, 1913, in a small tree about 12 feet from the ground. I lightly shook the tree and two or three young birds flew out of the nest. They stopped close at hand and I had a good look at one. A female amakihi approached and by scolding and fluttering about tried to lure me from the nest. Later I took down the nest. It overhung the steep valley side but was not carefully hidden. The larger trees above it hid it from the owls. This nest was quite different from the apapane's, built almost entirely of grass and fiber of the ieie vine and lined with rootlets and some sheep's wool. About 3.75 inches wide by 3.5 deep, the hollow at the top 1.75 inches.

The characteristic odor of the Drepanine birds was strong in this species. A bird flying past to windward left the odor plainly perceptible in the air.

OAHU AMAKIHI

Chlorodrepanis virens chloris (Cabanis)   Plate 11, Fig. 3

Endemic to Oahu. The bird survey (1935-37) found this bird not uncommon in the Oahu forests and it seems likely that it will survive indefinitely. I noted the habit of its going in small companies and of searching in folds of dead leaves for food.

ANIANIAU

Chlorodrepanis parva (Stejneger)   Plate 11, Fig. 2

Nianiau means *straight,* probably referring to the bird's straight bill. On Kauai the birds were sometimes confused with young amakihi under the name *Alawi* or *Aalawi.* We were given the name *Anauanii* for the bird. It seems appropriate, referring to the bird's habit of eating in small bites or nibbles.

Endemic to Kauai. This lovely little bird has upper surface bright yellowish olive green, underneath bright olive yellow. It is as dainty as its colors are pretty. It is one of the smallest of Hawaiian forest birds, about 4½ inches in length. In the 1890's it was extremely numerous all over the Kauai forest. It is still common in some localities but observers who are not acquainted with the Kauai birds might easily over-estimate its numbers by mistaking the young amakihi for it.

My notes say: "Their graceful movements and neat form with their yellow plumage places them among the prettiest birds in the Kauai forest." A bright lively bird, quicker in movement than Loxops. When larger birds chased it out of the flowering trees, it would as quickly return, sometimes almost at the tail of its pursuer. It generally gathers its insect food among the twigs and leaves but sometimes in the loose bark. It is very fond of visiting the koa flowers but we do not know what it gets there. From notes taken in February, 1891: "The koas came into flower about a week ago and are now about gone. The amakihi and anauanii had a lively time amongst them for a few days." It has a very sweet little song "befitting such a bird," my notes say. There were signs that the breeding season was approaching, (in March 1891). There seems to be no data on its nest, eggs or young.

GREEN SOLITAIRE

Viridonia sagittirostris Rothschild   Plate 12, Fig. 6

This species was apparently quite unrecognized by the Hawaiians, who had no name for it.

Bright olive green on upper parts, underparts yellowish green; wings and tail with green edges to the feathers. Length about 6.5 inches. Perkins' diary says: "I note that the maxilla is dark above and pale bluish white along the basal half, the legs and feet are slate color, the iris brown. There is a distinct crop or dilation of the oesophagus and the tongue is strictly drepanine as in the amakihi."

Endemic to the Island of Hawaii, "its habitat is limited to the dense forest a few miles in extent upon either side of the Wailuku River, at an elevation of from 2,000 to 4,000 feet." (Henshaw.) Palmer had discovered it in 1892 but Perkins did not know where he had collected it and was surprised to find it in December 1895 on the Wailuku river where he heard it call and thought it might be a mamo. He later spent two weeks in that excessively wet region and became well acquainted with the bird. It was rare but he saw as many as 12 one morning.

Perkins found it fed chiefly on crickets and a small caterpillar from the dry ieie stems. He describes its call as low and rather plaintive but it can be heard from a long way off, somewhat resembling an old native's imitation of the mamo call. He also says its song is very like that of the amakihi but it is louder and sometimes at the end there are one or two very powerful notes. The song is drepanine but distinct from the others.

The Creepers

There are 7 species and subspecies in the genus Paroreomyza. Henshaw referred to *Paroreomyza mana,* the species of the Island of Hawaii, as the Olive Green Creeper, so I shall designate all of them as creepers. The species vary in color but not greatly in habits. Most of them gather their food from the bark of trees.

KAUAI CREEPER

Paroreomyza bairdi bairdi (Stejneger)   Plate 12, Fig. 4
Hawaiian names: *Akikiki; Akikeke.* The name is probably an imitation of its quick chirp.

"Adult. Above hair-brown, tinged with pale green on rump and on margin of tail feathers. Below olive buff, nearly white on chin and throat, and tinged with pale yellow on the breast and abdomen. Lores whitish. Length about 4.45 inches." (Henshaw.) It is a little larger than the Hawaii species and has quite a different appearance, caused by its inch-long body feathers and white about the neck and face.

Endemic to Kauai, this interesting little bird's habitat is in the cold wet mountain tops from 3,000 feet upwards. We found few at lower levels but they were common at Kaholuamanu at over 4,000 feet elevation. At this elevation they went in small flocks accompanied by the ouholowai, the Loxops of Kauai. The akikiki hunts in the bark and Loxops in the foliage. The constant chipping of the akikiki attracted other birds and the groups reminded one of Bates' description of the birds in one part of the Amazon region in South America, where he found different species in numbers foraging in company. Following Francis Gay's advice, to find certain rare species we would follow the chipping of the akikiki and it helped us considerably. None were seen for certain in the survey, but Donaghho reported seeing it in 1941.

Their flights are short from tree to tree. They are active birds running under and over the trunks and branches and were equally adept in either position. Their food is principally insects and larvae which they obtain through a careful search of the crevices of bark and tree. They also take honey from the ohia flowers.

The chipping cry is very distinctive and though common to others of the genus it is more conspicuous in the Kauai bird. We found a large tapeworm in one.

OLIVE-GREEN CREEPER

Paroreomyza bairdi mana (Wilson)   Plate 12, Fig. 5

No Hawaiian name has been learned for this species.

Light green above, below green with yellowish tinge, wings and tail brown. Bill straight. Length about 4.5 inches.

Endemic to the Island of Hawaii, this little bird is inconspicuous compared with the species of Kauai. It was quite numerous in some parts of Hawaii and very scarce in others for no apparent reason. It is said to be still present though I did not see it in the survey. It does not go in small flocks like the Kauai bird, nor gather other species with it. It is quiet and inquisitive; if one stays still it comes quite close to make an examination. We found it difficult to distinguish from the amakihi but for its straight beak.

At the time we were in Kona it was feeding as were most other birds, on the ieie flower. Elsewhere it had insects and grubs in the stomach. Some had little but insects' eggs.

I noted that it seldom made the chipping chirp of the Kauai bird, but I heard one singing a very sweet little song.

I know of no observation having been made on its breeding habits.

PERKINS' CREEPER

Paroreomyza perkinsi (Rothschild)

This species was named by Rothschild from a single male specimen we collected at Puulehua, Kona, Hawaii, on September 25, 1891. Rothschild considered it to be intermediate between the creeper *(Paroreomyza mana)* and the Hawaii amakihi *(Chlorodrepanis virens)*, and thought that it might be a hybrid. Perkins thought it might be a sport.

MOLOKAI CREEPER

Paroreomyza maculata flammea (Wilson)   Plate 12, Figs. 1 & 2
Hawaiian name: *Kakawahie*. The name translates literally "to break up firewood," referring to the chipping call of the bird.

The male is mostly scarlet in shades varying on different parts. The female is brown with some scarlet markings. The immature males are in every stage between the female and the adult male. They are beautiful birds. Length about 5 inches.

Endemic to Molokai, and in danger of extinction, in the 1890's this beautiful bird was found in the upper boggy forest. I collected a series of specimens in 1907 when it was still quite common. It chirped like the Kauai bird and could be attracted by an imitation of the call and, being inquisitive, it fearlessly approached the human intruder. Their habit of searching in the bark was similar to that of the Kauai species. The survey disclosed no signs of it nor was its familiar chipping heard.

Perkins saw a young male being fed by its parent on June 10, 1893. He had previously found a young one with the down of the nestling still on it. Alanson Bryan described nests from one seen in May 1907 as follows: "It is made up of moss neatly woven together, and measures 4 inches in diameter by 2.75 deep. The interior is lined with blackish rootlike stems of dead moss and a few fibers from disintegrated ieie leaves. The bowl is just over 2.00 inches across by 1.5 deep."

There is little hope of saving this interesting and beautiful bird, unless it has a refuge, as I hope it has, with other Molokai native birds on the elevated plateau between Wailau and Pelekunu Valleys.

LANAI CREEPER

Paroreomyza maculata montana (Wilson)   Plate 12, Fig. 7
Hawaiian name: *Alauwahio*, or shortened to *Alauwi* or *Lauwi*.

Endemic to Lanai, and almost certain of complete extinction. The creeper of Lanai was yellowish green on upper parts, lemon yellow on under parts. Length about 5 inches. It was a neat little bird, and appeared to be smaller than the Kauai species.

It was formerly common in all parts of the Lanai forest, but has declined in late years with the other Lanai birds. A pair was seen in March 1937 but it had been scarce for some time before that. There seems little or no chance of its survival and it will probably share the fate that is inevitably in store for most, if not all, of the Lanai native birds. We cannot blame the introduction of foreign wild birds for this as almost no perching birds have been introduced to Lanai for a long time.

The habits of this bird are very like those of the other species: short flights, finding its food in the bark of tree trunks and branches, greeting the stranger with its chipping call, but using it more sparingly than the Kauai or Molokai species. Perkins described its song as vigorous and rather pretty. He saw it rise straight up in the air singing as some of the Hawaiian thrushes do. He collected young birds in July 1894. On April 19, 1913, I found a nest that had been blown out of a tree which I thought belonged to the Lanai creeper. It was different from the other nests I had examined. It was a neat little ball built compactly of very fine grass stems and skeleton leaves alternately, 1.75 inches across the bowl, .75 inch deep, sides .5 thick. Other nests were more ragged on the outside.

MAUI CREEPER
Paroreomyza maculata newtoni (Rothschild)
Hawaiian name: *Alauwahio.*

I thought this bird greener and less yellow than the Lanai species. Length about 5 inches. Endemic to Maui. I collected a few specimens for the Bishop Museum in February 1928. It was then not uncommon, and I saw a small group on the Kula pipeline trail in 1936, so it would seem it has a good chance of survival. Henshaw mentions its frequenting the underbrush more than the Hawaii species. He also mentions one singing, evidently to lure him away from its young which he was observing. Perkins noticed this trait of singing under excitement in the Lanai species.

OAHU CREEPER
Paroreomyza maculata maculata (Cabanis)   Plate 12, Fig. 3
Hawaiian name: *Alauwahio.*

Yellow and olive green are the principal colors of the Oahu creeper.

Endemic to Oahu. It was fairly common in the 1890's. I tramped many miles of newly made C.C.C. trails on Oahu in 1935 and did not see a single individual but other observers report having seen it since, commonly, thus promising a prospect of survival.

Its habits are much the same as those of the species of Maui and Lanai.

The Akepas
The interesting genus Loxops has 4 species; one each on Hawaii, Maui, Oahu and Kauai. Perkins found the natives gave the name Akepa for the species on all islands but Kauai. Akepa means sprightly and he cites the different species of Loxops as lively. I have studied only the Loxops of Kauai and Hawaii and I recognize them in the thick foliage where they feed by their deliberate gliding movement. They did not seem to me as sprightly as the iiwi and apapane. Perkins undoubtedly saw them

under circumstances different to what I did. There are a number of instances of this diversity of opinion in skilled observers, through studying the birds at different seasons and under different conditions.

A special feature of this genus which distinguishes it from all other members of the family is a tendency to a crossing of the tips of the mandibles, the lower mandible having its point turned to one side or the other, causing the bird to be cross billed. Henshaw was at a loss to account for this. Perkins is positive it is to facilitate working in the leaf buds for caterpillars and insects hiding there. My theory is its usefulness for removing scale insects from the leaves of the trees. Possibly it serves both purposes. I have found the shells of scale insects in their stomachs. They are essentially insect feeders and are seldom seen to visit flowers and then they may be after insects attracted by the honey. But they still retain the honeysucker's tongue, and some of the species may still feed on honey to some extent. I shall use the name Akepa as a common name for all the species.

HAWAII AKEPA

Loxops coccinea coccinea (Gmelin)   Plate 13, Fig. 3
Other Hawaiian names: *Akakane; Akepeuie.*

Adult males are scarlet, about 5 inches in length. Adult female is a greenish color above, lighter below with a yellow spot on the breast. One was slate green with a yellow tinge across the face below the eyes; a bright yellow patch on the breast and up on the throat, and very slightly smaller than the male. Immature male, greenish color above and light below, with gray across the face and around the eyes. Immature female, brownish green above, lighter below with a light yellow patch on the breast.

Endemic to the Island of Hawaii. We found it common in all the forests of that island. At Puulehua, Kona, in September 1891, at 4,000 feet we could get only males and a few immature individuals. At Honaunau some miles farther to the south and at a higher elevation we found females more plentiful than males. In February 1892, at the foot of the upper peak of Hualalai we found males and females. On the slopes of Mauna Kea about 5,000 to 6,000 feet elevation it was more plentiful than anywhere else. In the Kohala mountains our native hunters considered it a variety of the ulaaihawane. The survey (1936-37) found it in the vicinity of the Hawaii National Park and on the southern slopes of Mauna Kea. On June 2, 1943, Dr. V. G. Clark who had been recently on a trip to the top of Mauna Loa brought me a dessicated body of a small bird. On a ledge of the crater at 13,010 feet elevation there was a pool of water, frozen at the time, and around it were 7 dead birds. I was able to identify it as a female of this species by its crossed bill and what remained of its colors. The birds had evidently been blown 20 miles up the mountain side from the forest below in a windstorm and had taken refuge in the crater. Their habit of flying high into the air at mating time may have been the cause of this.

Seldom still, but deliberate in its movements, slipping through the foliage of the trees with nothing like the sprightliness of the iiwi and apapane which it resembles to some extent in color, once found there was little difficulty in securing the specimen. It stayed in one tree for a considerable time and took but a short flight when it left. Its movements and longer forked tail served to distinguish it in the foliage. At Honaunau when hunting these birds there was danger of stepping into one of the tree holes which abounded in the smooth pahoehoe (lava). These tree molds where the molten lava had flowed round the trunk of a standing tree were sometimes a foot or more in diameter and several feet deep. They were often fringed with ferns which completely hid them from view. It was necessary to keep one's eyes on the bird as it moved about in the tree and little attention could be given to the ground surface.

Insects, caterpillars and spiders furnished most of their food. These were mostly gathered from the foliage. Male and female call to each other with a low single and double chirp. A twittering sound is made when flocking with the young and at mating time. Two or three together will fly up into the air spirally, twittering constantly. Perkins describes the song as a short trill and says that the female sings more musically, but still more softly than the male.

The young were in first plumage at Puulehua in September 1891. On the northern slopes of Mauna Kea above Mana they seemed to be mating in February 1892. Nothing is known of nest or eggs.

MAUI AKEPA

Loxops coccinea ochracea Rothschild   Plate 13, Figs. 2 & 5
Other names: *Ochraceus or Maui Akepeuie.*

The male is mostly dark orange in color, lighter below; the female dark green above and light yellow below. Length about 4.5 inches. Perkins remarks on the different forms of plumage in the adult males: "these being distinctly red or yellow during or previous to the nesting season . . . There are, however, individuals more or less intermediate between the two forms. The most deeply colored examples approach very closely to *L. rufa* of Oahu."

Endemic to Maui. Though I made a careful search I did not find this bird in February 1928, nor did I see anything of it on the survey when on Maui in July 1936. However, it may still hold out in the large Maui forests.

The feeding habits are much the same as the other species; also their call notes and song which Perkins describes as a short trill and the call note as a low *kee-wit.* He said they rarely sang, but were constantly calling to each other.

On April 4, 1894, he collected a female ready to lay and "saw a pair on the ground getting material for their nest, the female pulling off the soft down covering the just springing fronds of the fern." On April 9, 1894, he saw a pair sporting on the wing, "rising up till they appeared mere specks in the sky. They did not descend for several minutes."

OAHU AKEPA

Loxops coccinea rufa (Bloxam)   Plate 13, Fig. 1
Other name: *Oahu Akepeuie.*

Adult male. Upper parts rufous orange with brownish wash; wings blackish brown, greenish orange on outer webs; below reddish orange, lighter on abdomen and lower tail coverts; length about 4.37 inches.

In a paper by Perkins included with his journal and referring to 1893 he says: "Before I left Waialua, Palmer and Wolstenholme, Lord Rothschild's collectors, arrived there and shared the mountain house with me and afterwards from there camped far back in the mountains. I stayed with them for some time in their tent and was present with Wolstenholme when he shot the male *Loxops rufa* which had not been obtained since Lord Byron's visit in 1825. There was a second specimen in company with this, probably a female, but though we heard it we did not get in sight of it, nor of any other specimen. After I left . . . Palmer and his colleague again camped for some time where the Loxops occurred but failed to find another. Some 10 years later I came across a pair far back in the forest in the Wahiawa district, but I had no gun with me at the time." It has not been reported since but may still survive in the more remote forest.

KAUAI AKEPA

Loxops coccinea caeruleirostris (Wilson)   Plate 13, Fig. 4
Other Hawaiian names: *Ou-holowai; Akekee.*

Upper parts greenish olive, a yellow spot on the crown; beneath, yellow; wings and tail brown. There is much variety in the coloring of individual birds, but unlike the other species in the genus there is little difference between males and females. Length about 4.5 inches.

Endemic to Kauai. We found this very interesting bird generally in company with the Kauai creeper but did not see it at as low an elevation as the latter. Their natural habitat is between 4,000 and 5,000 feet elevation but in stormy weather they come down to about 3,500 feet. They are generally in small flocks, slipping around quietly among the leaves in the foliage of the tall ohias. Their peculiar movements and longish forked tail easily identify them. Their flights are short, from tree to tree. I am not sure that I saw it in the survey but it has been reported as seen since. It stands a good chance of survival as it keeps above the range of disease-carrying mosquitoes.

Its food is insects, caterpillars, spiders' eggs, and scale insects. On March 25, 1891, we took 7 specimens from flocks above the Kalalau Valley. All were males but two and one of the females had ovaries enlarged.

The Akialoas and Nukupuus

The genus Hemignathus has two distinct species, *H. obscurus* and *H. lucidus*. The former are larger birds, have longer bills and not so much difference between the upper and lower mandibles. All gather their food to a great extent from the bark and wood of the forest trees. The two forms were known as Akialoa on Hawaii and the name Nukupuu was used on Kauai for the smaller form. I shall use akialoa as a common name for *H. obscurus* and nukupuu for *H. lucidus*.

HAWAII AKIALOA

Hemignathus obscurus obscurus (Gmelin)   Plate 14, Fig. 4

The Hawaiian names *Akialoa* or *Akihialoa* have reference to the long curved bill of the bird.

Plate 13

1. Oahu Akepa
2. Maui Akepa, male, red form
3. Hawaii Akepa, adult male
4. Kauai Akepa
5. Maui Akepa

Plate 14.

1. *Hawaii Nukupuu, female*
2. *Oahu Nukupuu*
3. *Oahu Akialoa*
4. *Hawaii Akialoa*
5. *Kauai Akialoa*
6. *Lanai Akialoa*
7. *Kauai Nukupuu*

(*All the birds pictured in this plate are undoubtedly
descended from a common ancestor species.*)

Upper parts bright olive green, duller on under parts, wings and tail brown. Length about 6.5 inches. Bill of male 1.85, of female 1.45 (Wilson).

Endemic to the Island of Hawaii, it is in danger of extinction. In 1891 it was well distributed over the Hawaii forests and common in Kona. My note on November 11, 1891: "At Nawina akialoa were plentiful sucking honey from the flowers of the low Clermontia trees." We saw them on the Kohala side of the Kohala mountains. In 1936 and 1937 I did not see any in Kau, Kona or the Kohala mountains and as far as I know none have been seen since.

The Hawaii akialoa gains its food by probing in crevices in the bark of trees, sometimes breaking off pieces of bark and dropping them. It probes under lichens and in the bases of the leaves of the ieie vine; it is also fond of honey from the flowering trees. Perkins remarks that when taking honey it seemed to sing more freely than at other times and conjectured whether the honey diet had the effect of stimulating singing. I have particularly noticed that when the iiwi and apapane were feeding on honey from the ohias they were exceedingly sprightly and wondered if it had a stimulating effect on them. With many birds going over and over the flowers each will get but a small taste from each flower and that might perhaps cause their haste. But again the birds at this time seem care-free and dash about and sing joyously when not seeking food. It is really a scene of merry-making; a scene I fear will never be replaced. Henshaw never saw this bird taking honey from flowers and he never heard it sing. This is another instance of trained observers seeing birds differently under different conditions. The Hawaii akialoa is easily distinguished by its call note.

Perkins once saw this bird's nest. "It was built towards the extremity of one of the largest spreading branches of a koa, placed above a fork and well concealed. It contained only one young one, and that already able to fly, while a second one was seen sitting on the branch outside the nest, with the old birds . . . The nest so far as I could get sight of it appeared to be quite similar in form to that of *Chlorodrepanis,* but was better concealed among the lichens covering the branch and these appeared to be partly used in its construction. This nest was found at the end of June and in the same district (Kona) many young birds were noticed at the time being fed by the parents."

LANAI AKIALOA
Hemignathus obscurus lanaiensis Rothschild   Plate 14, Fig. 6

Male: back olivaceous green, breast dirty yellow, under tail-coverts cream white. The one Perkins saw was more yellow. The bird I saw which may have been this species was very yellow. Rothschild's male was probably a young bird. Female: color dull grayish olive, more yellowish on abdomen.

Endemic to Lanai. Probably extinct. Wolstenholme collected several specimens of this bird for the Rothschild collection. Perkins saw one which he describes: "This was evidently an adult male, in plumage appearing quite brightly yellow and unlike any of the figures in Mr. Rothschild's work. There is no doubt that his figure of an adult bird, if really taken from an adult, represents the bird in its non-breeding stage, for in January, when I saw the one above mentioned all the adult birds on Lanai were in the fullest and most perfect plumage. It was extremely tame, at times not 5 yards distant, hunting for insects along the trunk and large limbs of a partly fallen ohia, which over-hung the edge of a precipitous cliff. As, if killed, it would necessarily have fallen in the brush far below or have lodged in the shrubbery on the side of the cliff, being without a dog I forbore to shoot, and when after some minutes it flew off, it was seen no more. It is probable that this was really a survivor of the brood obtained by Mr. Rothschild's collectors, since Wolstenholme, who discovered the bird, informed me that all of their specimens were obtained in the same spot and practically at the same time. Certainly the bird seen by me was quite alone, and this at a time when mature birds were all paired, and it may even be feared that it was the sole living representative of its species. If, however, a few pairs remained it is possible that the Lanai akialoa may even have increased in numbers, as I am told that the forests of that island have improved rather than deteriorated since I made my last visit." The forest certainly has improved but the bird has not been seen for a certainty since Perkins saw it. I watched for it for 20 years and on only one occasion saw a bird that might reasonably be supposed to be this species. It was across a small valley from my position, moving up the steep hillside, flying from tree to tree. It was more yellow in color than any other Lanai bird, about the size and with the action of an akialoa, but I could not say for certain that it was this bird. I made two collections of the forest landshells of Lanai, two botanical collections, and hunted goats all through the forest; I explored for water in its valleys and rode its bridle trails scores of times, but I never again saw a bird I even remotely thought might be an akialoa.

OAHU AKIALOA

Hemignathus obscurus ellisianus (Gray)   Plate 14, Fig. 3
Jibi (Wilson & Evans)

Other Hawaiian name: *Iwi or Iiwi.* This is a peculiar and surprising transference of the name, as the true *iiwi* is a distinctly different bird.

The plumage of this species is duller than that of the other species. At least the only specimen known to exist during the period Perkins was in the field showed this and he said of the ones he saw: "I distinctly noticed the somber plumage of the upper parts . . ." However, J. C. Greenway, Jr. in "The Auk" of April 1941, reviewing J. d'Arcy Northwood's "Familiar Hawaiian Birds" states: "Actually there are three specimens, one in Berlin and two in Leyden. They were collected by Herr Deppe in 1834."

In October 1892, Perkins was sure he saw a pair of these birds. He was then familiar with the *Hemignathus* of the other islands. I quote from his journal: "On a very narrow part of the ridge a pair of green birds flew across in front of me one just behind and in pursuit of the other, which squeaked as it flew. This darted across the ridge and down the Nuuanu side, the other alighted in an Ohia bush on the ridge, . . . I had no doubt at the time that this was the rare Akialoa of Oahu . . . On a number of days afterwards I hunted around Waolani, and once more I spent a night in the open on the ridge but never again saw anything that could be mistaken for a *Hemignathus.*"

Harold Craddock is sure he saw one of this species in 1937, and J. d'Arcy Northwood also at a later date as stated in the Preface of his "Familiar Hawaiian Birds." On both occasions the bird was taking honey from ohia flowers. Both are good ornithological observers and it is possible the bird may still exist. I, myself, collected a specimen of a bird on Lanai long after Perkins and Palmer had combed the little forest without finding any of the species. If still existing it is hoped that future observers may have a chance to study its habits as so little is known of this bird.

KAUAI AKIALOA

Hemignathus obscurus procerus Cabanis   **Plate 14, Fig. 5**

Other Hawaiian name: *Iiwi*. The true *iiwi* of Kauai was generally known as *Iiwipolena* (adult) and *Iiwipopolo* (young), or *Olokele*.

The plate gives a good idea of this remarkable bird. It seemed to me that in full breeding plumage the adult male was almost all yellow. Length 7.5 inches; bill of male 2.37 inches and female 2.12.

Endemic to Kauai and probably near extinction. We found this bird in all parts of the Kauai forest from the upper plateau to the forest edges near the seacoast on the north side. In all my visits to the Kauai forests since 1920 I have not seen or heard anything of this bird. Donaghho reported seeing it on the upper plateau in October 1941. It is hoped his observation is correct and that the bird will survive.

Active on its short legs, hopping along the branches and trunks of the trees, searching both sides of the branch in one trip, probing with its beak in holes and crevices in the bark and decaying wood, this is a most interesting bird. Its flights are short, from tree to tree, sometimes singing as it flies. It also searches the bases of the leaves of the ieie *(Freycinetia)* and halapepe *(Dracaena)*. Sometimes it descends to the ground to forage for grubs and insects amongst the dead leaves and possibly to pick up gizzard stones. The long honeyeater's tongue is useful in extracting honey from the deep tubes of the lobelia flowers and in working out grubs and insects from their hiding places. Its food is insects and larvae, cockroaches, insect eggs, grubs, caterpillars and nectar from flowers. They answer each other with a chirp, and also have a very distinct call much like a linnet's but a little louder. Both male and female have a light sweet song, the female with fewer notes than the male. In January and February, 1891, we did not notice their singing, but in March and April it was quite noticeable, and they also seemed to have a different chirp at Hanalei where we were in April, evidently a breeding season call. On April 20, 1891, I spent a day collecting with Mr. Francis Gay on our first hunting ground by the head of the Hanapepe Valley, Kauai. The koas were in flower and there were many birds. Gay wanted some oos for Wilson and Palmer had written me from Honolulu to procure specimens for some clients in England. We secured two akialoas out of several seen, one a beautiful yellow bird. All the birds seemed to be breeding at that time. Unfortunately for this study we then left for the Midway trip and did not return till the breeding season was over.

Although these birds were quite numerous, it was evident that they were susceptible to disease. Their habit of coming to the forest's edge and to low elevations exposed them to introduced diseases. One was so disabled with lumps on legs and bill that it could scarcely fly. Another had a tumor a quarter of an inch thick in its throat full of small worms, and a tumor on its ovaries containing a brown paste. Perkins found them with tapeworms. Its decline was likely starting at that time. It may survive at the higher elevations.

KAUAI NUKUPUU

Hemignathus lucidus hanapepe Wilson   Plate 14, Fig. 7

The Hawaiian name *Nukupuu* is very descriptive of the bird: *nuku*, the bill of a bird, *puu*, a small round hill.

Upper parts and breast gamboge yellow, white on abdomen; bill and feet slaty black. Length 5.6 inches. Upper mandible 1.2, lower .5. One bird was almost all yellow, the forehead being especially bright, another was slaty color with a few yellow feathers on the head. Female: breast primrose yellow, dull white on abdomen. The female is a much smaller and duller bird than the male. One had only one spot of yellow and that on the throat at the base of the bill. We collected 7 or 8 males to two females. The females are only distinguishable in the trees from amakihi by their long thin bills.

Endemic to Kauai, and probably near to extinction, the species was discovered by Wilson about 1887 at Kaholuamanu and named by him *hanapepe*. We seldom found it below 4,000 feet elevation. The species was not common and we would have taken few specimens but for its habit of accompanying the little flocks of akikiki whose chirping drew our attention and we followed the flock, thus obtaining this bird, akialoa and ou-holowai *(Loxops)*. Perkins also obtained a good series of skins. I took a specimen in December 1898, and two more on May 6, 1899, all males. I doubt if it has been seen since.

It was tame and unafraid, not seeming to notice our approach. It searched the bark and loose wood on living and dead trees. Its flights were short, from tree to tree. The two taken in 1899 were hunting their food amongst the leaves of rather low trees. They were quite tame and close together. I do not think we saw them hunting amongst leaves in the early part of 1891. At that time they were foraging in the bark only for grubs and beetles. On this occasion they were getting caterpillars from the green leaves. The birds collected as specimens had grubs and caterpillars in their stomachs, some of the caterpillars being over an inch long; others had remains of beetles.

In searching for food it would pause to utter its clear and distinct *kee-wit.* Perkins said its song was "a short trill," and that it was "fairly lavish of its song." One at Kaholuamanu had small sores on its feet.

OAHU NUKUPUU
Hemignathus lucidus lucidus Lichtenstein   Plate 14, Fig. 2

Above olive green, below yellow. Endemic to Oahu and probably extinct. There are few specimens in collections. Deppe took specimens about 1837 in Nuuanu Valley where it fed on honey from the flowers of the plantain. Perkins found evidence that it abounded in the Oahu forests in some numbers in 1860. None of the collectors in the 1890's found any trace of it.

MAUI NUKUPUU
Hemignathus lucidus affinis Rothschild

Yellow in different shades is the prevailing color of this bird. Endemic to Maui. Perkins found it more numerous than the Kauai species in the restricted areas it inhabited. He gave its habitat at from 4,000 to 4,500 feet elevation on the northeast slopes of Haleakala. Its habits agree very nearly with those of the Kauai nukupuu. Perkins remarked that it seemed to imitate the song of the imported linnet *(Carpodacus).*

This bird has not been seen since Perkins collected on Maui.

HAWAII NUKUPUU
Hemignathus lucidus wilsoni Rothschild   Plate 14, Fig. 1
Other Hawaiian names: *Akiapolaau; Akialoa; Akialoa nukupuu* (?).

"Adult male. Upper parts bright olive green, brighter on head and rump; wings and tail brown; underparts gamboge yellow."

Endemic to the Island of Hawaii. This remarkable bird was common in Kona during our collecting time there. Perkins found it widely distributed over the island, its range being above 3,500 feet level. I did not see it on the survey but it has been seen since, I think, in fair numbers near the Hawaii National Park. It is hoped that it will survive as it is an exceedingly interesting bird.

Its lower mandible instead of being curved like that of the other nukupuu is straight, the tip only contacting the upper mandible. All its muscles are well developed especially those of the head and neck and its skull exceptionally thick. The head is larger than that of the Kauai species and we had difficulty in getting the skin over it. The mandible seemed to extend further back than in most birds. I believe this has been brought about by its habit of using the lower mandible as a woodpecker does its bill. It uses great energy in beating at the bark and wood, breaking off pieces and dropping them. Perkins states that it strikes with the points of both mandibles at the same time. I watched them very closely, but without a glass, and was sure that the bird held the upper mandible out of the way and struck only with the lower which is stiff and strong and fitted for digging into the rotten bark and wood. With both together it seemed to me that it would not be nearly so effective. The bird frequently detaches pieces of bark and wood and drops them off the tree. As the bird still exists this is a question that can be fully examined by ornithologists. Perkins had greater opportunities of studying the bird than I had and his conclusions may be right, though we both may be correct. Perkins says that both the Maui and Kauai nukupuu make the tapping noise with their bills, though not so loud as the Hawaii species. I did not notice it in the Kauai bird. The remarkable thing about it is that in the Kauai nukupuu the lower mandible curves and is thin and in no way suitable, as I thought, for the woodpecker action as practiced by the Hawaii bird. My notes say: "It drives the lower mandible with considerable force into the crevices of the bark, the mouth kept open, the tapping noise being plainly heard at a distance, sometimes drawing our attention to the bird. When it gets the lower mandible inserted it uses it as a lever bearing both ways, using considerable force throwing its head from side to side. The pieces which break off it takes with both mandibles and throws off, sweeping the long upper one into the crevices opened on the branch."

In the latter part of September 1891, the parents were leading their young about, the latter seeming to depend on the parents for some time after leaving the nest. I saw a male and female tending a young one. Previously we had always seen only one young with either parent bird and had concluded that they shared the young, each taking one. The young one would sit fluttering its wings and chirping loudly, now and again trying to dig into the bark, but flying to the parent at the slightest chirp from it. On one occasion a female was near a young bird when a male flew to the latter and began to disgorge its food to the young one. Both were evidently attending one chick. I sometimes met the young alone. They were then very tame and inquisitive and if I stood still would come quite close to examine me. I saw an adult drive an akialoa out of a tree and preempt its claim. One was sampling koa pods, evidently hooking insects or grubs out of the half opened pods.

PSEUDONESTOR

Pseudonestor xanthophrys Rothschild   Plate 15, Fig. 5

Other name: *Parrot-billed Koa Finch.* The thick-billed Drepanids are not finches, and I think it inadvisable to continue the use of an incorrect name.

At first these birds, along with *Telespiza, Chloridops* and *Rhodacanthis,* all birds with heavy finch-like bills, were mistaken for finches, but as they were shown later to belong to the endemic Hawaiian family of the Drepanids and in no way allied to the finches, I see no point in continuing to call them such.

The genus Pseudonestor was erected by Rothschild to carry a remarkable bird discovered by Palmer on Maui. There are no woodpeckers or parrots in the Hawaiian group; but as the Hawaii nukupuu adopted habits and acquired somewhat the structure of woodpeckers, so did *Pseudonestor* develop characteristics and habits of a parrot.

Plate 15 gives a good idea of this bird. Its length is about 5½ inches. Immature birds are colored much like the adult but are pale yellowish underneath (Henshaw). Perkins thinks it is most nearly related to the nukupuu (*Hemignathus lucidus*) "which it resembles in its robust body and short tail but differs from that genus chiefly in the enormous development of the beak, which is of great size and compressed form affording a large surface for the attachment of the large muscles of the jaw which are necessary in performing its work; further in the loss of the typical tubular character of the tongue." It has also characteristics like the ou (*Psittacirostra*) and Perkins is of the opinion that it is intermediate between the two forms, the passage from the extremely slender beak of the nukupuu and the thick bill of *Pseudonestor* having evolved through another less exaggerated form now extinct. Endemic to Maui, Perkins, Palmer and

Henshaw found it rather a rare bird between 4,000 and 5,000 feet elevation on the northwest slope of Haleakala in the eighteen nineties. I failed to find it in 1928 in a very careful search, but was told by a workman of a bird he called "boring bird" seen when he camped with surveyors in the Kaupo Gap in the southwest corner of the crater of Haleakala. He said they came out of the main forest in the evenings to a small patch of trees in the crater. His description tallied with the action of this bird. This would indicate that it inhabited the forests of Hana and Kipahulu Forest Reserve and there is ground for hope that it may still survive. I traversed miles of new C.C.C. trails in the Hana forest in 1936 and though there was fairly good foraging ground in the large koas I saw nothing of the bird. The forests on the east and south sides of Haleakala have been little worked for study of the birds. It may remain indefinitely in remote recesses of that forest.

It was sluggish in action, tame and unsuspicious. In feeding it sometimes hung by its feet to a twig, brought its head over it and with its powerful bill split the twig over the burrow of the grub on which it largely fed, after the manner of a parrot. In hunting along the trunks of fallen trees it searched one side after the other as it proceeded like the akialoa and nukupuu.

This bird's food is mostly gained from the koa and consists of the larvae, pupae, and immature beetles of a native species; but it also visits other trees as *Pelea*, where it obtains the larvae of another native beetle and leaves remarkable scars on the tree. It feeds its young partly on these and partly on looper caterpillars.

The call note is a loud *kee-wit* very like that of the nukupuu with which it sometimes associates. Perkins once killed both Pseudonestor and a nukupuu with one shot. Its song is "quite similar to that of the latter, a short, vigorous trill, at its best fully as loud as the nukupuu of Hawaii." It sometimes sings when on the wing, but more often when feeding on the koas, pausing at intervals like the nukupuu to make its call.

Perkins once saw a nest of this bird; at least he said it could only have been of this species or the Maui nukupuu. It was well hidden, built among lichens which partly composed the material of the nest. It was of a simple cup-shaped form. Old birds, with young just able to fly, occupying the tree induced him to believe it was their nest.

DYSMORODREPANIS

Dysmorodrepanis munroi Perkins
Other name: *Hook-bill Lanai Finch.* No Hawaiian name is known.

Endemic to Lanai and nearly extinct. I discovered this bird on February 22, 1913, in the Kaiholena Valley. It flew from a tree with a little chirp and alighted a short distance away, and thinking it was an ou I shot it. It measured 6 inches in length, larger than *Pseudonestor* of Maui and smaller than the ou. It was molting and hard shot, and its sex could not be ascertained on dissection. Its color on the upper parts was light gray with a tinge of green. A light band ran along the wing showing on the side and there was a light mark over the eye; underneath lighter, almost white. Its striking peculiarity was its beak. Both mandibles were curved towards each other so that the tip of the lower is the only part that touched the upper leaving an opening between them like the Hawaii nukupuu, only more exaggerated.

I saw a bird of this kind on two occasions afterwards, once on March 16, 1916, farther up the Kaiholena Valley, and again on August 12, 1918, at Waiakeakua at the southwest end of the forest. On both occasions I was sure that it was not one of the known birds of the Lanai forest. The one at Waiakeakua showed distinctly the white mark over the eye, not on any other Lanai bird. The action and voice of the birds in both cases were different from any of the Lanai birds. But in neither case was I close enough to distinguish the shape of the beak.

I made a serious mistake by not saving the whole body in spirits for anatomical examination, or at least treating the tongue in this way. I dried the tongue which detracted from its value as a specimen. I should like to impress this on observers in the remote chance of their finding the body of some rare bird. The tongue is an extremely important diagnostic feature in the Drepanids.

On several occasions when on the lookout for this bird I heard a strange bird chirp, especially at Waiakeakua. It was generally on the wing as it sounded from different directions, now on this side, now on that. On every occasion I failed to catch sight of it. It is possible that the bird is not so rare as might be supposed. A quiet retiring bird, as this evidently is, might remain unnoticed a long time, even in a forest as small as that of Lanai.

It is my theory that this bird and the other rare Lanai bird, the Lanai akialoa *(Hemignathus obscurus lanaiensis)* both frequented the forest of akoko *(Euphorbia lorifolia)* that originally covered the plains now planted in pineapples. The akoko tree has fruit about the size of that of the opuhe *(Urera sandwichensis)* on which the bird was feeding when taken. As I understood from persons who remembered this forest it was a continuous area of thousands of acres of akoko trees.

I believe these two species had become adapted to this unique forest and when it was destroyed they became reduced in numbers while the other Lanai birds remained especially numerous, only to go down in their turn when conditions changed again. It was the irony of fate that they still survived in numbers when the upper forest was almost destroyed and then succumbed when their foraging ground had become vastly improved. There are several species of akoko in the Lanai forest and the opuhe also abounds in different valleys so the bird will find sustenance if it still survives.

I tried for several years to obtain another specimen so as to allay any doubts that might arise that this specimen is a sport but I failed to do so. From my experiences with this specimen and observations in the forest afterwards I am convinced that the species existed in the early years of this century.

OU

Psittacirostra psittacea (Gmelin)   Plate 15, Figs. 6 & 7
Other Hawaiian names: *Ou poolapalapa* (male) and *Ou-laueo* (female), indicating, respectively, the yellow-headed and the leaf-green ou. Wilson spells the second name *laevo*, which is obviously incorrect.

Two versions of the generic name of the ou are found in the literature, Wilson and Perkins spelling the name *Psittacirostra*, Rothschild and Henshaw using *Psittirostra*. Temminck, the author of the name, first spelled it *Psittirostra*, but later amended it to the correct grammatical form, which should be accepted.

With its yellow head and bright green body in varying shades on different parts the ou is a beautiful bird. The female lacks the yellow on the head and the immature are duller and also without yellow on the head.

Endemic to the main group but dangerously near extinction. In the eighteen nineties the ou was extremely common on all the forested islands except Oahu from which it had nearly disappeared. It seemed strange that it should disappear from Oahu and remain common on the other islands, but it has since disappeared from all the other islands as well.

The ou's habit of coming down to the lowest levels where food could be found, exposed it to introduced diseases, probably mosquito-borne. The introduced guava which covered large areas at the lower' levels proved a lure and the birds carried the diseases into the forest depths when they returned to feast on the ieie flowers and fruit, berries of the arborescent lobelias and other fruits of the uplands. On Lanai the bird was under my eye and I reported to the Bishop Museum every year. I quote from my 1923 report: "The forest birds of Lanai are holding their own and some species probably increasing, in the following order, ou, olomao, amakihi, apapane, *Oreomyza* and iiwi and there is every reason to believe that these species, with the proposed extension of the forest area planned by the Hawaiian Pineapple Company, will flourish indefinitely." A vain hope, for in 1932 I state in the report: "Lanai forests were often visited. The native birds though much more numerous than on Kauai or Oahu, are getting scarcer; the ou has not been seen for some time."

The ou was a high flier and migrated from one part of the forest to another. High winds carried them from island to island and so it kept uniform over the whole group. It was slow in its movements in the trees.

Perkins thinks that the inflorescence and ripe fruit of the ieie vine was its original food and that its parrot-like hooked bill was developed to facilitate its scooping up the fleshy flower bracts and picking the ripe fruit from the upright spadix. In the Pelekunu Valley Perkins complained that he could not find an untouched fruit of the mountain apple *(Eugenia)*. The bird had, however, a wide field in fruits of the introduced plants and trees. I found them feeding on guavas on Kauai and on mulberries on Hawaii.

The ou not only had beauty of plumage but it had a beautiful voice. Its song sometimes started with several clearly whistled notes that I thought were like those of *Rhodacanthis* but not so strong. It had a plaintive call and by imitating it the bird would answer and guide one to its quiet perch among the green leaves where it was scarcely visible.

There is no recorded instance of its nest or eggs being seen. Probably it was securely hidden in the masses of staghorn fern or ieie vines.

Its feathers were used in Hawaiian feather work.

Psittacirostra deppei Rothschild

Rothschild's collectors did not obtain the ou on Oahu but from older specimens Rothschild described the Oahu bird as different from the others. This does not seem likely as the common bird inhabited Kauai and the other islands to the southeast of Oahu and it seems likely that the birds in the eighteen-nineties were still being carried from island to island. The ou has been seen on Oahu by observers but no specimen has been taken for a long time.

PALILA

Loxioides bailleui Oustalet   Plate 15, Fig. 2

The name refers perhaps to the gray color of the bird. This name *Palila* has been applied to *Chloridops* through an error that crept into a paper by Perkins which appeared in "The Ibis" at a time when he was camped out in the wilds of Hawaii and was unable to check the proofs.

Neck, throat and breast yellow, rest of under surface dull white. Upper surface mostly ashy gray. The palila was rather a nice looking bird.

Endemic to the Island of Hawaii, it is now in danger of extinction. At about 4,000 feet elevation in Kona in September 1891, it was common, tame and easy to collect. Perkins found it common in Hamakua. But his journal on August 14, 1894, in Kona states: "The Palila *(Loxioides)* is now almost totally absent though at this season, 1892, it could be seen in numbers here every day and in all conditions of plumage. I have seen but two males on this occasion."

I found no signs of this bird in 1936, but Donaghho reported in 1937 seeing some high on the sides of Mauna Kea.

A sociable bird going in small companies. It feeds to a great extent on the seeds of the mamane *(Sophora)*, holding the pod down with its foot and tearing it open with its hooked bill. We found it feeding on poha fruit. I saw one eating the seeds of the naio*(Myoporum)*, cracking the nut with its bill like *Chloridops*. Evidently the seeds were green as the cracking sound was not nearly so loud as that made by the other birds when cracking the dry seeds. *Chloridops* occasionally eats the green seeds and it can be seen how it developed its strong bill by starting with green seeds. Perkins found it feeding its young on caterpillars and at times feeding heavily on them itself. He said it had a whistled call note to which it readily responded; he described the call as having an inquiring or inquisitive nature. I noted it had a low chirp and a very low song.

Perkins found it nesting in the Mamane trees in Kona at from 4,000 to 6,000 feet elevation in 1892. He saw young in all stages from some scarcely able to fly to nearly mature, but he found no nest with eggs.

Much as this bird has been reduced in numbers there is hope that it will survive at the higher elevations.

HOPUE

Rhodacanthis palmeri Rothschild   Plate 15, Figs. 3 & 4

Andrews' Hawaiian Dictionary lists *hopue* as the name of a fiber-yielding tree. Probably it is *Urera sandwichensis*, known today as *opuhe*, but I fail to see the connection between that and the bird. Perkins went to great effort to find the native names of this bird and Chloridops, but failed in both. I greatly doubt the validity of the name *Hopue.*

Mostly reddish orange in color, the full-fledged birds had a golden sheen over the head which faded out to some extent in the skin. With the exception of the crow, it was the largest of the perching birds of the Hawaiian forests, and one of the finest looking.

Endemic to the Island of Hawaii and now in danger of extinction. It was one of Palmer's discoveries. He found the first specimen on September 26, 1891, at Puulehua on the Greenwell ranch in Kona. Perkins found it afterwards in Kau. Henshaw failed to find it a few years afterwards in the region where Perkins and Palmer collected it. In the survey in 1937 the only trace I could find of it was from a guide in Kona who had heard a bird whistle a year or two before. His imitation of the whistle sounded to me identical to that of the bird as I remembered it. Donaghho reported he heard it whistle near the Hawaii National Park in 1937.

Undoubtedly descended from the same honey eating ancestors as other Drepanine birds, it long ago deserted honey for a vegetable diet. Finch-like characteristics were developed as with others of the group. According to Perkins its honey eater's tongue does not show as great a modification as do some of the others, the ou for instance. The bill has much the same structure as *Chloridops kona* but is more slender and with corners on the lower mandible. Unlike *C. kona* the head can be taken through the skin without difficulty. Their stomachs were large and the covering thin. We noticed a strong odor from the flesh.

It fed largely on the green beans of the koa. The first one I saw was hanging back downwards evidently working on a bean pod, after the manner of *Pseudonestor*, as described by Perkins. Old pods on the ground had a row of holes cut in them where the seeds had been. The seeds of these Hawaii koas were large and sometimes the birds' stomachs were stuffed with large pieces which had been cut up by their sharp-edged beaks. Some had a few smaller seeds in their stomachs and one small group was feeding in the low aalii trees *(Dodonaea)*. They made quite a rustling in extracting the seed from the dry shell surrounding it. Perkins found it occasionally feeding on caterpillars and feeding its young on them.

Its song or call is several whistled flute-like notes, the last ones prolonged. It seemed to flood the whole surrounding forest. We could find it only by its whistle, loud from the tops of the koas. That itself was difficult as the bird seemed to have ventriloquial powers and the whistle sounded from different directions. It required patience to secure the specimen.

We found the birds varying much in size and also, to some extent, in color. One or two were colored like the ou with yellow heads and green backs. These were afterwards described by Rothschild as a different species but as there were intergrades we did not consider them different.

We collected adults and young birds, apparently still with the parent, feeding on the koa beans. Ovaries of a female in one of these groups were enlarged as if she were preparing to have another brood.

Perkins saw the male bird come down to the ground for nest-building material and carry it to the top of a tall koa tree. Afterwards when the koa trees were more or less stripped of leaves by caterpillars he saw good-sized nests, probably of these birds.

Rhodacanthis flaviceps Rothschild

We were surprised to see that some of our "big finches" were classed as a different species. There is some doubt about the validity of this species and I shall quote from my notes to throw some light on this: "September 30, 1891. In the heat of the day I shot another of the great finches. It has a little yellow over its bill. It was feeding in a koa top. Palmer killed another at the same time, a much smaller bird with golden head and neck and light yellow breast. It was also in the koa. The tree has seed pods on it and it seems they are feeding on the seeds." October 1. "The male and female great finches of yesterday were 7.62 and 8.62 inches. Their stomachs contained mostly the seeds of the koa, the male having some smaller seeds." October 10. "The finches vary much in size, 2 adult males 9 inches, one 8.75, one young female 8.5, an adult female 7.5. Their colors also vary a good deal." October 13. "2 male giant finches 8.75 and 8.62, female 7.12 inches." October 16. "Palmer brought back some finches, one of which was colored very much like an ou; the head being yellow and the back and rump green." It might be noted that these measurements were taken in the flesh including all curves. Rothschild was, I think, at times puzzled with the difference between our measurements and that of the dried skins; but the difference is not at all surprising considering Palmer's system of measuring and of preparing skins.

Had we had the slightest suspicion that there were two species I would have taken more complete notes. They might, of course, be hybrids with the ou but this seems unlikely considering the habits of the birds. We saw no evidence of their mixing.

TELESPIZA

Telespiza cantans Wilson

The story of this species is told in "The Ibis" for 1890, p. 341. The schooner "Mary Bohm," Captain Bohm, Master, was heading for Honolulu in a more or less unseaworthy condition. A landing was made at an island (the story said Midway, but this could not be so. It must have been either Laysan or Nihoa). About 50 birds of this species were caught by the crew in the scrub covering part of the island. Another landing was made at Niihau, and Mr. George Gay, the manager of the island ranch, replenished the somewhat exhausted stores of the ship and the Captain gave him 10 of the birds and no doubt told him where he had obtained them. He sold the remaining 40 in Honolulu and Wilson succeeded in obtaining one of these and took it alive to England. He erected the genus *Telespiza* for it. He described it in "The Ibis" as stated above, accompanied by a colored plate of the bird. The other birds disappeared and probably all died.

Palmer on his return from Laysan gave a male specimen of the "Laysan finch" to the Gay and Robinson collection. On April 23, 1892, Francis Gay told me that Wilson's specimen came from Nihoa and was different from the Laysan bird. George Gay had left Niihau for California in 1891 or early in 1892 and visited with his people, the Gays and Robinsons at Makaweli, Kauai, when on the way. He no doubt noted the difference between the Laysan specimen and the birds given him by Captain Bohm and told his brother Francis the story of the birds. I took employment with the Gay and Robinson Company after George Gay had gone to California. I made a note of what Mr. Gay told me and forgot about it for half a century.

If what Francis Gay told me is a fact, and I see no reason to doubt it, Rothschild's species *T. flavissima* is the Laysan bird, and *T. cantans*

applied to it in an article by Perkins in "The Ibis" and, following him, by Henshaw, is an error.

Most of plumage olive green, dull white on abdomen. Length about 6 inches. Endemic to the Island of Hawaii and occupying an area of about 4 miles square, though Palmer did see a pair at Honaunau about 10 miles farther along the side of Mauna Loa, southward, this interesting bird is now in danger of extinction. It was discovered by Wilson in June 1887, when he obtained two specimens. Palmer collected a good series of specimens in September 1891, and Perkins also in 1892 and '94. Palmer searched for the bird for about a week before he found it but once found, we became familiar with its habitat and we procured our specimens easily. It frequented the naio (*Myoporum*) trees and in breaking the hard dry seeds with its strong heavy beak made a cracking sound which guided us to it. Perkins never saw more than 6 or 8 in a day but Palmer on one occasion collected 12 in one day. Five of these were together and 10 of them not more than 100 yards apart. It seldom strayed from the more recent aa or clinker lava flows. These areas were covered with medium-sized trees and little undergrowth. In working over this rough, jagged loose rock we wore out a pair of shoes in a very short time. It might be supposed that a bird with a bill so large in proportion to its size would find it inconvenient to carry, but this bird hopped about in the trees carrying its bill with neck outstretched with perfect ease. Perkins found it a sluggish bird but I thought it active at times. When feeding it did seem sluggish, it sat still and cracked nuts but it could move about with considerable alacrity. We found considerable difficulty in getting the skin over its large head and strong jaw muscles. Its food was almost entirely the little maggot-like germ from the center of the naio seeds but sometimes it cut up the green nuts and swallowed them. It also ate green leaves and at times caterpillars.

A small squeak and a light sweet song are the only call notes recorded. A low cheep repeated at intervals. The song is sometimes long with a variety of notes. It sang more vigorously when excited, on one occasion when it lost its mate. It has not been seen since Perkins collected it in the eighteen-nineties. Henshaw failed to find it and considered our wonderful collecting area, which we thought a collector's paradise, one of the poorest over which he had hunted. It can be seen from some of Perkins' experiences how quickly the birds disappeared from some localities.

There is a remote possibility that it will survive on some of the rough lava flows at a high elevation.

Stray Visitants to the Hawaiian Islands

To see and identify any of the stray visitants involves a much greater element of fortuitous luck than is present in the rewards of studying the resident birds. The bird student must accept the records of others and feel elated if he sees for himself a few of those listed as stragglers or chance arrivals, or can add a new one to the list.

Casual observations are to some extent uncertain and great care must be taken to be sure of the species. For instance: I have a wide experience with the akialoa of Kauai, yet in 1936 after watching a bird in a tree above me with a field glass for a considerable time I almost erroneously noted it as an akialoa. It was a young iiwi in the greenish yellow of its first plumage. Its color and actions were like those of the young akialoa sucking honey from the flowers of the ohia tree.

As an aid to observers in identifying the straggling birds listed, I have based very brief descriptions on the "Marks for Field Identification" in "The Game Birds of California," and many of them are taken from that work (GBC). Descriptions adapted from other works are noted by the name of the author in parentheses.

PHALACROCORACIDAE   Cormorant Family
PELAGIC CORMORANT
Phalacrocorax pelagicus pelagicus Pallas

"Head and neck violet black with changeable reflections; rest of body greenish . . ." (Henshaw.)

A specimen of this species was taken by Schauinsland on Laysan Island in 1896. Henshaw relates that a pair of cormorants came to Hilo Bay in November 1900, and stayed till the spring of 1901. He thinks they were possibly of this species.

ARDEIDAE   Heron Family
REEF HERON
Demigretta sacra (Gmelin)

"General color dark slaty grey, darker on the upper surface, tinged on the lower surface with brown . . ." There are two forms, a pure white and the ordinary slaty blue one. (Oliver.)

Henshaw states: "Dr. Finsch who was well acquainted with the bird in the islands further south, is quoted by Rothschild as stating that he observed the white form once at Kahului, Maui." I saw a pair of these birds in 1938 at Rose Island near Samoa. There were two together, one pure white and the other of the slaty blue form. I once visited a nesting place of this bird in the Hauraki Gulf, Auckland, New Zealand.

Rose Island is not so far from Hawaii but that one might straggle to Maui.

THRESKIORNITHIDAE   Ibis Family

WHITE-FACED GLOSSY IBIS
Plegadis guarauna (Linnaeus)

"Curlew-like profile; bright iridescent chestnut colored plumage appearing black at a distance . . . down curved curlew-like bill about 5 inches in length . . . and long legs. Fly in orderly diagonal lines with legs and neck extended." (GBC.) Length about 24 inches.

There are a number of instances of this species visiting here from the mainland. Knudsen obtained a specimen on Kauai in 1872, and G. P. Wilder shot one, probably of this species, in 1873. I preserved a fine specimen on Molokai in 1903. John Fleming told me of seeing several ibises together in the 1930's. C. S. Childs of Wailuku, Maui, reported 3 at the Kanaha pond on that island on November 18, 1937.

ANATIDAE   Duck, Goose and Swan Family

LESSER SNOW GOOSE
Chen hyperborea (Pallas)   Plate 5, Fig. 14

This species is marked by "Large size, pure white body plumage, black flight feathers, and reddish bill and feet . . . Immature birds also appear white at a distance." (GBC.) Length about 27 inches.

A specimen of this goose was taken on Maui by Brother Matthias Newell. One was reported from Oahu in 1904.

AMERICAN WHITE-FRONTED GOOSE
Anser albifrons gambelli Hartlaub   Plate 5, Fig. 9

Identified by "Large size, white forehead, black speckled belly, reddish feet, light brown bill and general gray body color . . ." (GBC.) Length about 28 inches.

Palmer secured a male of a pair of this species from a lagoon at Honokahau, near Kailua, Hawaii, in December 1891. Comparing it with the Hawaiian goose which we were collecting at the same time, it was seen to be lighter in color, of a shorter and heavier build, bill much larger and flesh colored, legs and feet finer, of a bright orange color and fully webbed. Its gizzard was much larger, indicating that its food was of a more solid nature than that of the Hawaiian goose. It measured 27 inches in length. There was one in my collection that was taken at Kaunakakai, Molokai in 1905. I have been informed of other straggling geese which I feel sure were of this species. It seems a fairly frequent visitor to this group.

EMPEROR GOOSE
Philacte canagica (Sewastianov)

"Medium size and short neck. Head and neck, (except throat) white, plumage ashy blue barred with black, tail white tipped, bill and feet light colored." (GBC.) Length about 27 inches. A straggler of this species was reported from Puna, Hawaii, in 1903. A goose probably of this species landed in Makaweli, Kauai, in 1940.

BLACK BRANT
Branta bernicla nigricans (Lawrence)

"Moderately small size . . . with very dark coloration. Head and neck black, with white collar about front of neck, sides of rump white, bill and feet black. Flies in undulating course, close to water." (GBC.) Length about 23 inches.

A specimen obtained by Palmer from Mr. Newell which was collected at Kahului, Maui, in 1891, established this species as a straggler here in Hawaii. My brother, James G. Munro, reported 3 of these birds on Molokai on February 23, 1938. They stayed on the southeast coast of that island for some time.

CACKLING GOOSE
Branta canadensis minima Ridgway   Plate 3, Fig. 5

Identification marks are "Similar to those for Canada Goose but size considerably smaller . . . In hand the tarsus is seen to be much longer than the middle toe with claw, while the bill is less than 1.44 inches long . . . The high-pitched call-note is easily distinguished from the Canada and Hutchin's geese." (GBC) Average length 24 inches. Marks for identification for Canada goose are: "Very large size . . . black head, neck, bill and feet, white cheek patches and uniform-appearing gray body . . . Recognizable in flight by abruptly black head and neck, gray body plumage, loud trumpet-like 'honks' and slow wing strokes."

Palmer secured a specimen of this goose from the lagoons at Mana, Kauai, in March 1891. Rothschild, not knowing that mainland geese straggled to these islands, described it as a new species and kindly complimented me by calling it *munroi* but discovered his mistake later. In December 1902, a cowboy on the Molokai ranch, Molokai, by a lucky shot hit one of these birds in the neck with a rifle ball as it was flying past. There are other instances of this bird having been seen on these islands.

MALLARD DUCK
Anas platyrhynchos platyrhynchos Linnaeus   **Plate 5, Figs. 1 & 2**

"The large size . . . metallic green head, white ring round neck, and violet colored speculum identify the male. The violet or purple speculum bordered along both edges with black and white distinguishes both sexes in all plumages . . . except . . . the natal. In flight the white under wing-coverts show forth. The female can be distinguished from the Black Duck, a near relative, by its much lighter color." (GBC.) Length over 22 inches.

We were told of mallards migrating here when we collected in 1891 but did not see any that we could identify. Schauinsland secured an adult male on Laysan Island in July 1895. Perkins reported it from Oahu and Molokai and shot one himself. Some are kept on private ponds on the islands. Most breeds of tame ducks are descended from this species.

GREEN-TAILED TEAL
Anas crecea carolinensis Gmelin

"Very small size . . . male chestnut brown head with green patch back of eye, white bar across side of breast and bright green speculum bordered above and below by black . . ." (GBC.) Male averages 12.25 inches in length; female smaller.

Perkins mentions this species as known to sportsmen as an occasional visitant. There are 3 recorded instances of this beautiful little teal straggling here. To Maui, 1892, Laysan, 1896 and Molokai, 1906. I collected the specimen from Molokai at Palaau of that island. There were large mud-flats out in the bay and small lagoons inshore where the migratory ducks congregated.

J. d'Arcy Northwood records in "Familiar Hawaiian Birds" that in January 1940 a flock of 14 was seen on Oahu.

BALDPATE

Mareca americana (Gmelin)   Plate 5, Figs. 10 & 11
Other names: *Widgeon; American Widgeon.*

"Medium size, white axillars, and more or less white on forepart of wing. Males have top of head white, sides of head mixed black and white, a green patch behind eye, green speculum, white flank patch, and black under tail-coverts. Both sexes distinguished from European widgeon by pure white rather than gray axillars and male by lack of reddish brown on head . . . The wings make a whistling noise when the birds are in flight." (GBC.) Average length 19 inches.

Schauinsland obtained a specimen on Laysan Island in 1896 and I took one on November 3, 1902 at Palaau, Molokai. Northwood states in "Familiar Hawaiian Birds" that a flock of 15 was seen on Oahu in January 1940.

GADWALL DUCK

Chaulelasmus streperus (Linnaeus)

This rare visitor can be recognized by its "Slender appearance, long pointed wings, general gray coloration, and pure white speculum . . . under tail-coverts black in male." (GBC.) Average length 20.5 inches.

Perkins mentions this duck as "noticed by sportsmen as rare immigrant." I collected a specimen at Palaau, Molokai, on November 11, 1902.

BUFFLE-HEAD

Bucephala albeola (Linnaeus)

"Small size, chunky build, relatively large head, short bill, black (or dark) and white coloration, white patch on side of head, and white speculum separate either sex from other ducks. Female slightly smaller than male, with much of black replaced with blackish brown; distinguished by white patch on side of head behind eye, and white wing patch crossed by a black bar." (GBC.) Average length of male about 14.75 inches.

Perkins mentions this chance migrant as reported from Oahu, Maui and Laysan. Northwood in "Familiar Hawaiian Birds" states that a flock of 12 was seen in January 1938 and 4 in November 1929 on Oahu.

WESTERN HARLEQUIN DUCK
Histrionicus histrionicus pacificus Brooks

"Size medium . . . bill very small, tail short and pointed, general coloration very dark, below as well as above. Male has several conspicuous white patches on sides of head and body, as also a white collar around hind neck, a white bar across side of chest, and a white patch on wing. Female dull brown with dull white spots on head, the most conspicuous one below and behind eye, no white on wing. Females of both Bufflehead and Oldsquaw have white streak directly behind eye." (GBC.) Length about 17.75 inches.

E. H. Bryan, Jr. notes a chance migrant reported on Laysan in 1906.

RED-BREASTED MERGANSER
Mergus serrator Linnaeus

"Smaller than American Merganser . . . Male: Reddish brown band across breast, and two black bars across speculum. Female: Cinnamon brown of neck not abruptly ended and back brown tinted rather than blue-gray. Both sexes have head crest of two points, one behind the other, and nostril nearer base of bill than middle . . ." (GBC.) Average length both sexes 22.5 inches.

Perkins reports this occasional visitant as well known to some sportsmen, and as having been reported from several of the islands.

LESSER SCAUP DUCK
Nyroca affinis (Eyton)   Plate 5, Figs. 5 & 6

"Not distinguishable from Greater Scaup at gunshot range. In hand, or within a few yards, the smaller size, purplish instead of greenish gloss on the head, somewhat coarser or more distinct black undulations on back and flanks, and lack of whitish on outer webs of innermost primaries identify the male Lesser Scaup. Females can be definitely distinguished only by size differences. The Lesser Scaup averages nearly 2 inches shorter than the Greater Scaup and is proportionately smaller throughout." (GBC.) Average length of male 17.25 inches. Female is smaller.

On November 11, 1914, a group of 4 of this species (as determined by E. H. Bryan, Jr.) settled in the reservoir at Koele, Lanai. I collected specimens to prove their identity.

CANVASBACK

Nyroca valisineria (Wilson)   Plate 5, Figs. 7 & 8

"Large size, reddish brown head and neck, canvas colored back and low forehead sloping down to long slender bill . . . Distinguished from Redhead by larger size, especially of the head, blackish coloration around base of bill, red iris, and sloping forehead and bill (which meet without evident angle between the two)." (GBC.) Average length, both sexes 21.75 inches.

Perkins mentions this species as a stray visitant. We were told of canvasbacks being among the other ducks at Mana, Kauai. My notes mention seeing them but I cannot say we positively identified them as we had then little experience with the migratory ducks.

GREATER SCAUP DUCK

Nyroca marila (Linnaeus)

"Medium size, stout build, dark-colored head and neck, broad 'blue' bill, conspicuous white speculum, and white under surface. Male Greater Scaup distinguished from male Lesser Scaup in hand by larger size, greenish instead of purplish gloss on head, and by tendency to white on outer webs of innermost primaries. Female Greater Scaup separable from all other ducks (save Lesser Scaup and Ringneck) by conspicuous white area encircling base of bill. Female Greater Scaup distinguished from female Lesser Scaup only in hand, by larger size and by tendency to white on outer webs of innermost primaries; from Ringneck by greater size and by gray instead of white speculum." (GBC.) Average length of male 19.25 inches.

Perkins mentions this species as a stray visitant. I might mention that during the ten years Perkins studied the Hawaiian fauna he was in close touch with a number of sportsmen of the old school who did a great deal of shooting when migratory birds were plentiful and stragglers often accompanied them. He thus obtained much information that other collectors missed.

ACCIPITRIDAE   Hawk and Osprey Family

MARSH HAWK

Circus cyaneus hudsonius (Linnaeus)

"General description. Length 19 inches . . . Males have the fore and upper parts light ashy, and abdomen white; females are dark umber-brown above and brownish white below. Both sexes have the face encircled with an imperfect ruff . . ." (Birds of America)

Wilson reported the presence of this hawk on Oahu.

AMERICAN OSPREY

Pandion haliaetus carolinensis (Gmelin)

"General description. Length 2 feet; spread of wing 4½ to 5½ feet; upper parts dark brown; head and under parts white" (Birds of America).

Dole recounted seeing this species on the coast of Niihau. Observers have reported it in recent years on Oahu, especially one at Salt Lake which stayed there for some time. I saw on October 16, 1920, on the east coast of Lanai a bird answering this description. It was sailing back and forth inland at a good height with little movement of its wings which I judged to have a spread of about 6 feet. It floated overhead in one place for a considerable time while I examined it with a field glass. Eventually it flew out low over the water and along the coast.

Straggling hawks are reported from time to time but it is difficult to identify them. On Niihau in November 1939 I saw a hawk harrying a small bird probably a skylark high into the air. It kept below its quarry forcing the small bird to fly even higher till when tired it would begin to descend, when the hawk could pounce on it. We did not see the finish but I had seen skylarks so hunted by the harrier *(Circus approximans)* in New Zealand, and have had descriptions of the Hawaiian hawk hunting birds in the same way. The hawk was too far away to permit even a guess at the species.

CHARADRIIDAE   Plover Family

BLACK-BELLIED PLOVER

Squatarola squatarola (Linnaeus)

"Moderately large size . . . Big head, short, stout, black bill, strikingly black axillars . . . Almost white upper tail-coverts, and short white band on spread wing; in addition in spring, black under parts, except for

abruptly white lower belly and under tail-coverts, together with the
absence of any golden color on upper surface. Voice: A loud ringing
'wher-rell' of a distinctly mellow quality." (GBC.) Average length
12.55 inches.

Reported from Hawaii in 1900 by Henshaw, and in recent years by
Northwood on Oahu, and by Donaghho on Midway.

KILLDEER
Charadrius vociferus vociferus Linnaeus

Identified by, "Moderate size, two black bands across chest, white collar
around hind neck, white bar across wing, tawny rump patch, and white
tipped black banded tail. The shrill call *kill-dee*, is distinctive. This is
our only shore bird with two black bands across breast." (GBC.) Average
length about 10.2 inches.

This plover has been reported as a chance migrant to Maui.

SCOLOPACIDAE   Snipe and Sandpiper Family

PACIFIC GODWIT
Limosa lapponica baueri Naumann

This bird is easily recognized by its long legs and very long slightly
upturned bill. Its winter plumage such as it would be in if straggling
here, is mostly brown or ashy brown with varying shades and markings.

There was a specimen of this species in the Gay and Robinson collection in 1891. One is in the St. Louis College collection, Honolulu, now
in the Bishop Museum. Schauinsland secured specimens on Laysan in
1896, and Helen Shiras Baldwin tells of one seen at Hilo.

The reason why this interesting migrant, which nests in the same
regions as the Pacific golden plover, does not include Hawaii in its regular
migration, is probably because it procures its food on tidal mudflats and
there are few such foraging grounds on these islands.

WILSON'S SNIPE
Capella delicata (Ord)
Other name: *Jacksnipe.*

"Medium small size, long bill, longitudinally striped head and back
(at all seasons), mottled breast, white belly, dusky rump, erratic flight,
sharp grating note, crouching attitude and solitary rather than flocking

habits; frequents grassy meadows rather than open mudflats or shores."
(GBC.)

This occasional migrant is reported on Hawaii by Perkins and by
E. H. Bryan, Jr. on Oahu, Maui and Laysan. I collected one at Palaau,
Molokai in 1902.

SHARP-TAILED SANDPIPER
Erolia acuminata (Horsfield)

"Adult in winter plumage. Above grayish brown, streaked and striped
with dusky; superciliary stripe and lower parts dull white; chest and sides
of breast, pale grayish buff. In summer the upper parts are brighter with
rusty and black; under parts streaked with dusky, and with grayish brown
V-shaped marks." Length 8.25 inches. (Henshaw.)

Henshaw tells of Schauinsland taking one on Laysan, A. F. Judd one
on Oahu, Brother Matthias one on Maui, and I took one at Palaau, Molokai,
in 1902. This sandpiper is probably a frequent visitor here.

PECTORAL SANDPIPER
Erolia melanotus (Vieillot)

"Medium small size . . . short bill about as long as head, white chin,
buffy foreneck and breast finely streaked with dark brown (this area
constituting a broad rather abruptly outlined, pectoral band), and blackish
rump and upper tail-coverts. More common on meadow land and less so
on open flats than other sandpipers." (GBC.) Average length about
8.81 inches.

Henshaw recorded two specimens taken by Mr. Hewitt at Kau, Hawaii.
Reported also from Oahu.

PHALAROPODIDAE   Phalarope Family
RED PHALAROPE
Phalaropus fulicarius (Linnaeus)

"Small size, chunky form, absence of spotting, streaking or barring
on under surface, white bar across wing, under surface chiefly reddish
brown in spring, with white cheek-patch, mixed white and dull red in
fall, and pure white in winter; neck short and thick (thicker than in
Northern Phalarope); wings not markedly in color from back; spends
much time in swimming on water, and, within our borders, is rarely if at

all, found feeding on shore; 'spins' about rapidly from time to time while feeding on surface of water." (GBC.) Length of male 7.9 inches; female larger.

This bird has been reported from several islands. One was given me at Makaweli, Kauai, in November 1896. During 1941 a number were seen to have migrated here. Four at least were picked up dead on the windward coast of Oahu. All were preserved as specimens and were found to be very thin though in good feather. It would seem that they cannot find the sustenance they require in our waters and die of starvation. These birds are easily mistaken for the akekeke (*Arenaria interpres interpres*) when flying over the water.

NORTHERN PHALAROPE

Lobipes lobatus (Linnaeus)

"Small size, needle-like bill . . . slender head and neck, white under-surface, and, in summer plumage, absence of conspicuous streaking or barring on back of head and back, and reddish sides of neck. Frequents open water, either salt or fresh; swims gracefully and with quick movements. Among Phalaropes, distinguished by smaller size, short slender bill, dark rump, and in summer plumage by blackish head and back. The phalarope most commonly met with on inland waters." (GBC.)

On March 15, 1893, a note in my journal says: "Mr. Gay showed me a peculiar little bird that young Knudsen had shot at Mana where he had seen a pair of them." The skin had been roughly prepared but I took a careful description of it and am sure it was this species. The tips of the slender bill were hooked, but this had evidently been done by pressure in skinning.

LARIDAE   Gull and Tern Family
RING-BILLED GULL

Larus delawarensis Ord

"Mantle pearl gray; lower parts white; bill greenish yellow, black banded near tip. Length about 18.2 inches." (Henshaw.)

Alanson Bryan reported an immature specimen in the collection at the St. Louis College, Honolulu. Another was secured by Mr. G. P. Wilder near Kaunakakai, Molokai on February 1, 1901, during a southerly storm. Bryan describes it as an immature winter specimen with the head and neck white.

HERRING GULL

Larus argentatus smithsonianus Coues

"General description—Length 24 inches. Color, pure white with grayish blue mantle." (Birds of America.)

E. H. Bryan, Jr. in his check list records a "Chance arrival (Laysan)."

CALIFORNIA GULL

Larus californicus Lawrence

"Mantle dark gray; bill yellow with a crimson spot near end of lower mandible; scalpulars and secondaries broadly tipped with white. In winter head and neck broadly streaked with brown. Length about 20-23 inches." (Henshaw.)

A specimen of this species mounted by Brother Matthias is in the collection of the St. Louis College, Honolulu. Reported by Alanson Bryan.

FRANKLIN'S GULL

Larus pipixcan Wagler

"Head black, with white on eyelid; mantle plumbeous; quills bluish gray, white tipped. In winter similar, but head white. Length 13.50-15 inches." (Henshaw.)

Alanson Bryan reported a specimen of this gull in the St. Louis College collection, mounted by Brother Matthias.

GLAUCOUS-WINGED GULL

Larus glaucescens Neumann

"Mantle pearl gray; head and under parts white; primaries with small white spots at the tips; in winter top of head and hind neck streaked with dusky. Length about 25 inches. The young are more or less variegated with white." (Henshaw.)

Henshaw reported this species as an occasional visitor to Hawaii. Schauinsland reported it from Laysan, and E. H. Bryan, Jr. lists it on Oahu.

POINT BARROW GULL

Larus hyperboreus Gunnerus
Other name: *Glaucous Gull*. Hawaiian name: *Koleaaumoku*.

"Head, neck, tail and underparts white; mantle pale pearl gray. In winter, head and neck streaked with brownish. Length about 25-28 inches." (Henshaw.)

There was a specimen of this gull in the Gay and Robinson collection in 1891. I saw one on the beach at Mana, Kauai, on March 18, 1891. I saw one on Hawaii in 1936 and have had a number of reports of its being seen at Hilo and on Maui. On December 30, 1931, I found one on the beach at Manele, Lanai. It was in good plumage but so thin and weak that it could not rise from the sand. It had the remains of a crab in its stomach. A flock of four or five had been reported on the coast of Lanai some time before and I saw the remains of one on the shore. The birds I saw were probably immature. This gull is evidently a frequent visitor here but for some reason does not thrive. The Hawaiians knew it as Mr. Gay gave me its Hawaiian name.

BONAPARTE'S GULL
Larus philadelphia (Ord)

"Head plumbeous; mantle pearl gray; underparts white; feet orange red. Adult in winter has a white head and flesh colored feet. Length 12-14 inches." (Henshaw.)

Palmer took a specimen of this bird at a lagoon at Polehale, Mana, Kauai, on March 14, 1891. This seems to be the only instance of this species being recorded here.

PACIFIC KITTIWAKE
Rissa tridactyla pollicaris Ridgway

"Head and neck white in summer, in winter crown and sides of head streaked with dark gray and back of neck gray like the back; underparts, under surface of wings and slightly forked tail white; mantle pearl gray... bill greenish yellow; feet dusky. Length 15.5-16 inches." (Alexander.)

There seems to be only one instance of this bird being identified in the Hawaiian group and that at Laysan.

ARCTIC TERN
Sterna paradisaea Pontoppidon

"General description. Length 14 to 17 inches. Color, pale bluish gray, lighter below." (Birds of America.)

This wonderful traveller which nests far north in the Arctic and migrates to the Antarctic experiencing a maximum of daylight hours, has been recorded from Hilo Hawaii, and Oahu. Included in E. H. Brayan, Jr. check list.

Plate 17

1. *Golden Pheasant, male*
2. *Golden Pheasant, female*
3. *Pea Fowl, male*
4. *Pea Fowl, female*
5. *Silver Pheasant, male*
6. *Silver Pheasant, female*
7. *Chinese Pheasant, male*
8. *Chinese Pheasant, female*
9. *Guinea Fowl, white*
10. *Guinea Fowl, pearl*
11. *Lady Amherst's Pheasant, male*
12. *Lady Amherst's Pheasant, female*
13. *Japanese Blue Pheasant, male*
14. *Japanese Blue Pheasant, female*
15. *Button Quail*

BLACK-NAPED TERN

Sterna sumatrana sumatrana Raffles

"Head and neck white, with a triangular, black spot before the eye and a black band on the nape; mantle and rump pearl gray; outer web of first primary black gray; tail long, deeply forked, white, the central feathers grayish . . . underparts white with a rosy tinge; bill black with a yellowish tip; feet black." (Alexander.)

E. H. Bryan lists this bird as reported from Hawaii and Kauai.

ALCEDINIDAE   Kingfisher Family

WESTERN BELTED KINGFISHER

Ceryle alcyon caurina Grinnell

"Adult male. Above bluish plumbeous; tail with transverse white markings primaries with spots of same; forehead with white spot, below white, with band of plumbeous across breast; white of throat encircling hind-neck. Female similar, but sides and flanks rufous, with interrupted band of same across belly. Length 11.00-14.5 inches." (Henshaw.)

Henshaw reported the presence of a pair at the mouth of Hakalau Gulch on the Island of Hawaii, in November 1901.

Imported Birds

The first and most obvious association of the term "imported birds" in the mind of the Honolulu public is a recollection of a trip to the Kapiolani Bird Park where imported rare tropic birds, prisoners of beauty, fill the eye with spectacular color, odd forms and strange habits.

A smaller public recalls trips across the island to the Bird Farm where imported birds, mostly game varieties, were bred in thousands before December 7, 1941, for release throughout the islands for entomological economy and as game for the hunter.

However, the one phase of the imported bird which comes closest to the every-day life of the community is the release of the domestic birds to brighten garden, shore, and hills, filling the void caused by the disappearance of the Hawaiian endemic birds.

For the restocking of the country-side with birds suitable for this climate and food supply the community is largely indebted to the Hui Manu.

PHALACROCORACIDAE   Cormorant Family

CHINESE FISHING CORMORANT

Phalacrocorax carbo sinensis (Shaw and Nodder)

General color a shining greenish black.

After Scott B. Wilson made his last trip to these islands in 1896 he went from here to Japan. When there he procured one of these birds and sent it alive to the Gay and Robinson family at Makaweli, Kauai. They did not have facilities for keeping it and released it in the sea at Makaweli. It was not heard of again.

PHOENICOPTERIDAE   Flamingo Family

FLAMINGO

Phoenicopterus ruber Linnaeus

General color in full plumage scarlet, generally lighter. Longs legs and long neck. Length about 4 feet.

Caum relates that Mr. H. D. Sloggett introduced 3 from Cuba to Kauai. They lived about a year there.

ANATIDAE   Duck, Goose and Swan Family

MUTE SWAN

Cygnus olor (Gmelin)

Plumage white. Length about five feet.

As related by Caum in "Exotic Birds of Hawaii" Mr. W. H. Wise about 1920 brought some to Hilo and released them near the town where they seem to be established.

MANED GOOSE

Chenonetta jubata (Latham)

General color brown and black on different parts. Breast black speckled. Length about 20 inches.

A few imported to Oahu in 1922 did not survive.

BLUE-WINGED TEAL

Anas discors Linnaeus

Above variegated with light and dark brown. Below different shades of gray. Conspicuous is a large white crescent with black edges, in front of eye. Length 16 inches.

Reported to have been imported in 1922 by the City and County of Honolulu from Australia. This is an American bird, and it seems hardly likely to be exported from Australia. More probably the birds in question belonged to one of the native Australian species of teal, and were wrongly identified. They failed to become established.

FALCONIDAE   Falcon Family

FALCON

Falco sp. indet.

Two birds, probably of this genus, which were being taken to Japan from Vancouver, B. C. escaped from a ship in Hilo Harbor. One was killed. I have no information on what became of the other.

CRACIDAE   Curassow Family

CURASSOW

Crax rubra rubra Linnaeus

A rather large bird about 24 inches long.

Imported from Panama in 1928 as a game bird but not known to be breeding.

GUAN
Penelope purpurascens aequitorialis (Salvadori and Festa)

About 35 inches long. Similar to the domestic fowl.

Imported as a game bird from Panama in 1928 but apparently not taking hold.

CHACALACA
Ortalis garrual cinereiceps Gray

A game bird resembling a Chinese pheasant. Brought to the Island of Hawaii as were the two former in 1928 from Panama.

TETRAONIDAE   Grouse Family
SHARP-TAILED GROUSE
Pediocetes phasianellus columbianus (Ord)
Other name: *Pin-tailed Grouse.*

"Medium size . . . unbanded, pointed tail . . . mixed color pattern of pale effect, on upper surface and pure white ground of under surface." (GBC.) Length about 17 inches.

Caum reports that about 30 were brought from the mainland to the Island of Hawaii in 1932.

PRAIRIE CHICKEN
Tympanuchus cupido americanus Reichenbach

"Differs from the Sharp-tail in being conspicuously barred on the under surface, and in bearing long blackish tufts of feathers on each side of the neck." (GBC.) Length about 16.5 inches.

Caum is not certain that this is the species of which Mr. A. S. Wilcox released 12 on Oahu in 1895. It is also supposed to have been liberated on Kauai. It has not become established on either island.

PHASIANIDAE   Pheasant, Quail and Partridge Family
MOUNTAIN QUAIL
Oreortyx picta palmeri Oberholzer

"Large size . . . long slender black plume, and bands of black, white and chestnut on sides of body . . ." Call note easily distinguishable from that of the Valley Quail." (GBC.) Length average 11.1 inches.

Imported from the mainland to Hawaii and Kauai in recent years.

CALIFORNIA VALLEY QUAIL

Lophortyx californica vallicola (Ridgway)   Plate 16, Fig. 9

"The short, blunt ended black topknot . . . in association with the scaled pattern of markings across lower breast is distinctive . . . From the Mountain Quail the valley species is known by smaller size, shorter, blunt-ended topknot, and presence of scaling on the belly, and from the Desert (Gambel) Quail, by absence of rich chestnut on sides, and presence of scaled pattern across lower breast." (GBC.) Average length 10.3 inches.

This species was early brought to the islands and in the 1890's was very common on Hawaii and Molokai. I saw a number on Kauai in 1936 and on Niihau in 1939. A very small importation to Lanai did not succeed. On Hawaii they were common in the open forest at 5,000 feet elevation. On Molokai they were in very large flocks in the algaroba forest along the coast line. They were tantalizing sport. A large flock would keep on the ground running along about out of range. When fired upon they rose and alighted on the tops of the thick foliage where they were quite out of sight. They would fly out one after another with loud whirring of wings but still unseen as the hunter came under the tree. The valley quail is a vegetable and insect feeder; seeds, green leaves and buds are in its dietary. In Kona we found them feeding on the fruit of the poha *(Physalis peruviana)* which was common in the open forest at 5,000 feet elevation. The egg clutch is large and the eggs very much spotted. The chicks fly when very young.

A species of bird malaria was found in this bird in the Hawaii National Park. (Paul H. Baldwin's report to the Superintendent, dated August 2, 1941.)

GAMBEL'S QUAIL

Lophortyx gambelli gambelli Gambel
Other name: *Desert Quail.*

Similar to Valley Quail, as regards size and crest, but general coloration much lighter; male with back of head bright reddish brown, and with a clear buffy white band across lower breast, followed by a conspicuous black spot on fore part of belly. Both sexes have the sides rich chestnut, but no scale-like feather tippings on the under surface of the body as in the Valley Quail." (GBC.) Average length 10.9 inches.

Established on Kahoolawe from introduction by Mr. H. A. Baldwin in 1928.

BOB-WHITE

Colinus virginianus virginianus (Linnaeus)   Plate 16, Fig. 8

Above chestnut mixed with black, tawny and grayish brown. Below brown with black and white markings, chestnut on sides. Length 10 inches.

Imported from Eastern States to Island of Hawaii and appears to be establishing itself there.

CHUKAR PARTRIDGE

Alectoris graeca chukar (Gray)

Above brownish olive to ashy, with red markings; below ashy to buff. Length about 15 inches.

Native of India. Introduced to Oahu, Molokai and Kahoolawe, and established on the two latter islands.

HUNGARIAN PARTRIDGE

Perdix perdix perdix (Linnaeus)

On upper surface color pattern is mixed, brown in various shades predominate; below white, black and chestnut cover most of the surface. Length about 12.5 inches.

Introduced a number of times to these islands but not known to be established on any of them.

PAINTED QUAIL

Coturnix coturnix japonica Temminck and Schlegel
Other names: *Chinese or Japanese Quail.*

Upper surface color pattern mixed, chestnut, black and white, belly lighter. Length about 6.25 inches. A male specimen I prepared on Lanai on February 7, 1928, measured 7½ inches; had bill black with base and nostrils brown; legs and feet cream, soles lighter, claws gray; iris light brown. It and another that had been killed by a telephone wire had dandelion heads, grass and weed seeds in their crops and stomachs.

Released on Maui and Lanai in 1921, it quickly established itself. Running in the long grass its calls can be heard for some time without it's being seen. The birds rise suddenly, fly a short distance and drop down into the cover. They go singly or in small coveys.

I saw a nest of this bird at Kapaa, Kauai on April 23, 1940. It was a hollow in the grass. There were two or three fresh eggs in the nest,

1.25x1 inch, ovoid, brown with numerous irregular large black blotches and streaks and smaller ones of a lighter shade. A mowing machine passed over the nest and the bird flew out from almost under it. It did not return, and abandoned the nest.

PECTORAL QUAIL

Coturnix pectoralis Gould
Other name: *Eastern Stubble Quail.*

Brown, white and black markings predominate on upper surface. Below lighter. Length about 7.5 inches.

Introduced by Maui County in 1922 from Australia. Released on Maui and Lanai. Those on Lanai did not persist or possibly hybridized with the Chinese quail, though no evidence of this is apparent in the Chinese quail at present on Lanai.

BUTTON QUAIL

Excalfactoria chinensis chinensis (Linnaeus)   Plate 17, Fig. 15
Other names: *Painted Quail; King Quail.*

Male. Above brown with black and buff markings; throat black, buff and white, belly chestnut. Length about 4.5 inches.

Brought from the Orient to Kauai in 1910 and established there. Brought later to the other islands, it does not seem to have succeeded.

I am told it is established on Oahu.

RED-CRESTED WOOD PARTRIDGE

Rollulus roulroul (Scopoli)

Male. On head a frontal tuft of long black bristles and on occiput a full hairy maroon crest, between them a white band; above dark green with bluish tinge; below mostly black. Length about 10.5 inches.

Introduced from Singapore in 1924 to Oahu, but did not establish itself.

SILVER PHEASANT

Gennaeus nycthemerus Linnaeus   Plate 17, Figs. 5 & 6

Head and lower surface purplish black, white marking on breast; above white with crescent-shaped black markings on back. Length about 40 inches of which the tail takes 24 inches.

Introduced early and recently. Native of southern China.

MONGOLIAN PHEASANT

Phasianus colchicus mongolicus J. H. Brandt

Male. "Length about 36 inches, the tail 22 inches; head dark iridescent green; a white collar around the neck, interrupted in front; mantle, shoulders, chest, and breast bronze red with purple and green reflections; lower back and rump dark iridescent green to purple; chin and throat purplish bronze red; chest, breast, and flanks tipped with very dark green; middle of breast and sides of belly dark green . . ." (Caum).

An early introduction but does not seem to have persisted in a pure form. To what extent it has hybridized with the ringneck is not known.

CHINESE PHEASANT

Phasianus colchicus torquatus Gmelin   Plate 17, Figs. 7 & 8

Other name: *Ringneck Pheasant.* Hawaiian name: *Kolahala,* a name that is very descriptive. It derives from *kola,* the tail of a cock, and *halaoa,* to project or to stretch out. A variant of this name, *kolohala,* is frequently used. Although the difference in pronunciation is slight, the difference in meaning is great. *Kolo* is to crouch, and refers to the way in which the bird crouches to hide.

"Marks for field identification—size of body between that of a grouse and quail, but tail feathers greatly elongated. Male with black appearing head, white collar, bronzy breast, black-spotted yellow sides, and with narrow sharp bars of black on tail. Female predominantly brown colored, slightly scaled on back, but uniformly pale brown on breast." (GBC.) Females of some species of pheasants are remarkably similar in color and markings. Length of male about 33 inches, tail about 18 inches.

An early introduction, well established on most of the islands, on Lanai it was especially numerous and furnished excellent sport when the large upper lands were in pasture. Hunting in the Ford car with or without a dog was good sport. Without a dog the pheasant crowed in response to the burring of the car and extended its head above the brush. The car was stopped but left with engine running. The sportsman fixed his eye on the spot as the bird ducked, and walked up to it. As the bird rose he had as good a shot as if hunting with a dog. When with a dog, he rode on the running board and jumped off from the slowly running car when he winded a bird. This area is now in pineapple fields and the hunting is not so good. One cannot help looking back and regretting the loss of the lure of those wide open spaces.

This bird's feeding habits were remarkable. It fed on one article of food at a time if sufficient were available to fill its crop. I examined many crops; they might be crammed with dandelion heads, sweet potatoes, guava fruit, pigeon peas, leaves of certain plants, cockroaches, caterpillars, etc. I know of no other gallinaceous bird that sticks so persistently to one kind of food at a time.

The nest is on the ground. The hen bird sits so closely that she can be easily caught at night on the nest. A certain amount of moisture is necessary for the hatching of the eggs and in an extra dry season few chicks were hatched—a provision of nature, as there would be little food for them if they were hatched. The eggs are brown and the clutch fairly large.

When wire fences were first erected on the upper plains of Lanai, pheasants were frequently killed by striking the wires. The birds were easily run down by the cowboys on horseback. If followed closely by the horse, they tired, seldom took a second flight and were easily caught in the long grass. A dog became smart at catching them by following the bird in the same way. Rules against these practices were soon made.

JAPANESE BLUE PHEASANT

Phasianus colchicus versicolor Vieillot   Plate 17, Figs. 13 & 14
Other name: *Japanese Green Pheasant.*

Iridescent green and purple are the predominant colors in the plumage of the male of this pheasant. Length about 27 inches.

An early introduction and later importations followed but the pure species does not seem to have taken a firm hold. It has hybridized with the Chinese pheasant and probably so lost its identity. Some were taken to Lanai but did not survive. It was later decided by the owners not to introduce more but to keep the Chinese pheasant pure there. I doubt if the Chinese pheasant on Lanai has any mixture of other species at present.

COPPER PHEASANT

Syrmaticus soemmeringii (Temminck)

General plumage of male largely chestnut with markings of black and other admixtures. Length about 50 inches, the tail taking about 37 inches of this.

Introduced from Japan and released on several islands but has apparently not remained a pure strain.

GOLDEN PHEASANT

Chrysolophus pictus (Linnaeus)   Plate 17, Figs. 1 & 2

Male. Head and rump golden, cape plumes on head orange, barred with blue-black. Wing brown, purple, chestnut and black. Length about 40 inches.

An early introduction, and also recently.

LADY AMHERST'S PHEASANT

Chrysolophus amherstiae (Leadbeater)   Plate 17, Figs. 11 & 12

Male. Head bronze green with blood-red crest; white cape over back of head and neck marked with black glossed with steel blue. Color pattern of body much varied. Upper parts green and black; most of underparts white. Length about 50 inches with tail of 36 inches.

Imported in 1931 and 1932 but not known to be established.

PEA FOWL

Pavo cristatus Linnaeus   Plate 17, Figs. 3 & 4

Peculiar crest, blue of head and neck, back bronzy green, below green and black, and a long sweeping train with eye spots on ends of feathers are the main features that meet the eye in this beautiful bird. Full length to end of train up to 90 inches.

Native of India and Ceylon.

Said to have been introduced by Mrs. Francis Sinclair in 1860. These birds are quite a sight on Niihau at this time. Unfortunately they were moulting when I rode over the island in 1939. I saw signs of them and heard their cries in the Kalalau Valley on Kauai in 1936. Charles Gay brought them from Kauai to Lanai and they were there in small numbers till Lanai City was built when they disappeared.

NUMIDIDAE   Guinea Fowl Family

GUINEA FOWL

Numida meleagris galeata Pallas   Plate 17, Figs. 9 & 10

An odd looking thickset bird with a bony helmet on its head, and white-speckled plumage on a grayish surface.

Early introduced but have not become adapted to conditions on these islands. Some released on Lanai in 1914 died out. Large numbers were released from the Game Farm a few years ago on several islands. I saw them shortly after on Lanai and Kauai and they did not seem to be doing well.

The call of the guinea sounds like "come back, be quick."

The nest is on the ground. Sometimes over a dozen shiny brown eggs are laid, with very hard shells.

MELEAGRIDAE   Turkey Family

TURKEY

Meleagris gallopavo gallopavo Linnaeus

Hawaiian names: *Palahu* or *Pelehu*. Both names refer to the soft, elastic bare red skin about the head and neck, which is puffed out and distended in the mating display.

Most of the body plumage is of a shiny bronze, copper and green. A long caruncular growth hangs over the beak and a tuft of stiff bristles hang from the breast. Length about 4 feet.

The turkey has done exceptionally well, probably on all islands, in a semi-wild condition. In connection with bird diseases I have been told that where numbers were very large many would suddenly die. On some islands the turkeys in a wild state were developed into an industry by snaring them on their roosts and shipping to Honolulu alive. One process of catching was simple. The catcher went out in the afternoon and spotted where the turkeys went to roost. On dark nights he went out with a home-made torch of sacking and tar, a long bamboo pole, and several long fish lines noosed at the end. The torch was lighted near the roost. As the gobblers craned their necks staring at the light the trapper with the pole slipped a noose over the head of each gobbler and then pulled all in at once. The birds were caught unhurt.

TURNICIDAE   Bustard Quail Family

PAINTED QUAIL

Turnix varia varia (Latham)

Above mixed color pattern; below lighter.

Introduced to Maui in 1922 but likely not successful in establishing itself.

GRUIDAE   Crane and Heron Family
LITTLE BROWN CRANE
Grus canadensis canadensis (Linnaeus)

"Large size, standing about 3 feet, long neck and black legs, and general bluish gray coloration without any contrasted markings; forehead unfeathered in adults; neck straight out in flight . . ."

Listed by Bryan as an escapee from captivity or chance migrant.

RALLIDAE   Rail Family
INDIAN BLUE GALLINULE
Porphyrio poliocephalus (Latham)

Blue in different shades are predominant features in this bird's plumage; under tail-coverts white; bill, frontal plate and legs red.

Native of southern Asia introduced through San Francisco in 1928. Not a successful introduction as far as known.

AUSTRALIAN GALLINULE
Porphyrio poliocephalus melanotus Temminck   Plate 2, Fig. 5
Hawaiian name: *Alae awi*. This is the bird known to the Maori of New Zealand as *Pokeko*. The name *alae awi* more properly belongs to a form of *alae keokeo* which has the frontal knob chocolate brown instead of the usual delicate pearly white. The reason for the transference of the name to this foreign bird is not clear, as the two birds are not sufficiently alike to be confused, especially by such close observers as the Hawaiians.

Large bill, frontal plate and long legs red; around head black, upper parts and tail brown, breast blue, under tail-coverts white.

An early introduction. At one time apparently established, but not much in evidence in later years.

LARIDAE   Gull and Tern Family
SILVER GULL
Larus novae-hollandiae Stephens

Mostly white, back gray; bill, legs and feet red. A very beautiful bird. Escapee from Honolulu zoo in 1924, but apparently did not survive.

It is a remarkable fact that gulls do not thrive here. This bird in New Zealand is remarkably adaptable and hardy and there seems no reason why it would not succeed here. A number of species of gulls straggle here but none has succeeded in establishing itself.

WESTERN GULL

Larus occidentalis Audubon

Mostly white. Bill yellow.

Has been introduced several times from the mainland but has not succeeded.

COLUMBIDAE   Dove and Pigeon Family

ROCK PIGEON

Columba livia Gmelin

Other name: *Wild Pigeon*. Hawaiian names: *Manuku; Nunu* (from its call).

Variable in plumage, although most individuals are slaty gray, a reversion to original form of rock pigeon.

An early introduction, the bird probably escaped from domestication but took to a wild life readily. It was in immense flocks on Hawaii in 1891; also on Molokai in the early nineteen-hundreds. It is valued on Lanai as a spreader of Australian saltbush seed, digesting the berry and sowing the seed.

PERISTERIDAE   Turtle Dove Family

MOURNING DOVE

Zenaidura macroura (Linnaeus)

Grayish blue above with shades of olive brown; below purplish with shades of buff and bluish on parts. Length about 12 inches.

Introduced from the mainland about 1930. Not known to be established.

INDIAN RING DOVE

Streptopelia decaocto (Privalszky)

Upper parts light brown and ashy gray on wings; below, breast pale lilac gray and slate. Length about 12 inches.

Introduced in the nineteen-twenties to Oahu and Kauai. May be established.

CHINESE DOVE

Streptopelia chinensis (Scopoli)   Plate 16, Fig. 6
Other names: *Lace-neck* or *Ring-neck Dove*. Hawaiian name: *Ekaho,*
very evidently from its call.

Largely grayish brown, neck spotted, tail white tipped except middle
quill.

An early introduction. A fine game bird in its flights. Well established
on all islands where there is growth of weed seeds. Not harmful unless
in spreading seeds of noxious plants. Few of the later introductions of
different species of doves have succeeded in establishing themselves in
competition to this well established species. The barred dove is an exception and it will be interesting to see to what extent it will displace this
species.

This dove breeds early and probably has successive broods. Its nest
is a flimsy structure of a few twigs. The eggs are white.

BARRED DOVE

Geopelia striata striata (Linnaeus)

Upper parts, neck, breast, sides and flanks thickly barred with black on
a grayish ground; breast reddish, lighter on the belly. Several individuals
measured from 8¼ to 9 inches in length, most of them 8½ inches. The
sexes differ very little if at all.

There has been considerable confusion in the identity of the little
Australian ground doves present in Hawaii, and it is very probable that
the original importations of 1922 consisted of several closely allied species
which were not at the time recognized as different. It is likely that this
subspecies is the bird recorded by Caum as "red-breasted doves" under
Geopelia humeralis. Aside from the Chinese dove, it was the only common
dove on any of the islands visited during the bird survey of 1935-'37,
although it had only recently been taken to Hawaii. It reached Lanai
unaided, probably from Maui, and until I took a specimen I thought it
was *G. tranquilla* reestablishing itself. This species had disappeared from
Lanai in 1928-'29. Specimens collected on Lanai in 1936 were identified
at the American Museum of Natural History as *Geopelia striata striata*
from Indo-Malaya. There are records that *G. humeralis* and *G. tranquilla*
were imported at the same time, but what probably occurred was that the
shipment actually consisted of *G. striata* and *G. tranquilla*, mixed. If
G. humeralis was represented as well, it evidently did not persist.

The barred dove is so small and tame it is not well received as a game bird. Sportsmen fear its competition will be detrimental to the Chinese dove, a favorite game bird, but this has so far not been demonstrated. It is an acquisition from an esthetic point of view as it is so tame on the lawns and sidewalks.

Large numbers seem to migrate from the coastal region of the islands for food or nesting, but these migrations have not yet been fully studied.

The nest like other doves is lightly built of twigs. The eggs are white, oval in shape.

PEACEFUL DOVE

Geopelia striata tranquilla Gould   **Plate 16, Fig. 1**
Other name: *Blue-eyed Dove.*

Upper parts and upper breast thickly barred with black on a grayish ground; throat pale gray; lower breast pale fawn running into whitish on abdomen; sides and flanks not barred as in *G. striata striata*; bill and bare skin of face and round eyes blue; legs and scales brown, between scales gray.

Introduced from Australia in 1922 by the City and County of Honolulu and Maui County. Mr. David Fleming representing the latter sent some of this species with a number of other birds to Lanai. This species was the only one of the consignment to establish itself there and it became numerous by 1926. Its calling could be constantly heard at Koele about half a mile from Lanai City. In 1926 I collected two specimens that had been choked by smoke from a brush fire, and thus the species could be definitely identified. Early in 1928 it almost disappeared. One was heard calling in August of that year at Maluea several miles from Lanai City, and again in April 1929 one was heard at the same place. There is no record of its being seen or heard since. The question arises why did they disappear? Did that consignment of birds bring a disease with them? I think not or they would not have thriven and multiplied for 6 years. Nor were they likely to have tried to migrate. The most likely solution that I can see is that a disease was brought to Lanai City which killed off this bird and the birds of the Lanai forest. The specimens I took of this bird and those of *G. striata* are in the Bishop Museum. They stand as evidence that both birds had inhabited Lanai.

BAR-SHOULDERED DOVE
Geopelia humeralis (Temminck)   Plate 16, Fig. 3
Other name: *Zebra Dove.*

Throat and face gray, upper surface brown barred with black. Under parts reddish, white on belly.

As mentioned before, this species has been confused with *G. s. striata.* Cayley in "What Bird is That?" says the cry of *humeralis* resembles "Hollyhock," which is like the cry of the small dove that is so common here. His plate of *humeralis* is also very much like our bird but I think larger. It is possible if *humeralis* succeeded in establishing itself that it bred with *G. s. striata* and so lost its identity. If a cabinet specimen were taken of every species when introduced and every decade succeeding if successfully established, we could collect a great many interesting facts. Changes could be noted as time went on.

DIAMOND DOVE
Geopelia cuneata (Latham)   Plate 16, Fig. 2

Head, neck and underparts gray, lighter on belly; upper parts spotted. Naked skin round eye red.

Several importations were made of this little dove from Australia. It was probably in the consignment from Maui to Lanai in 1922. It does not seem to have established itself on any of the islands.

GREEN-WING DOVE
Chalcophaps indica (Linnaeus)

"Head, breast and shoulders brown with iridescent lights . . . back and rump brown black crossed by two grayish bands, iridescent green between; tail brown black; abdomen lighter purplish gray; bill red; feet and legs pink." (Caum.)

Introduced from Singapore to Oahu in 1924. Not likely established.

BRONZE-WING DOVE
Phaps chalcoptera (Latham)   Plate 16, Fig. 7

Upper parts grayish brown, under pinkish; head and throat with varied markings of white, yellowish and gray; bronze and green spots on wing. Brought from Australia to Oahu in 1922, but did not survive.

Plate 19

1. *Non-pariel Bunting—male*
2. *Non-pariel Bunting—female*
3. *Indigo Bunting—female*
4. *Indigo Bunting—male*
5. *White-eye*
6. *Pekin Nightingale*
7. *Japanese Tit*
8. *Japanese Bluebird*
9. *Mocking Bird*
10. *Chinese or Wah Mee Thrush*
11. *Skylark*
12. *Shama Thrush*
13. *Willie Wagtail*
14. *Dyal Bird*
15. *Magpie Lark*
16. *Mynah*

CRESTED PIGEON

Ocyphaps lophotes (Temminck)   **Plate 16, Fig. 4**
Other names: *Crested Bronze-wing; Australian Crested Dove.*

Introduced from Australia to Oahu, Molokai and Lanai, but did not succeed.

Grayish brown in plumage lighter below; long black crest on head; bronzy marks on wing.

PLUMED PIGEON

Lophophaps plumifera (Gould)
Other names: *Spinifex Pigeon; Plumed Bronze-wing.*

Cinnamon is the prevailing color of this bird, underparts mostly white; varied markings on wings; a cinnamon elevated crest.

From Australia to Maui and Lanai in 1922. Did not survive.

PARTRIDGE PIGEON

Geophaps smithi (Jardine and Selby)
Other names: *Smith's Partridge Bronze-wing; Naked-eyed Partridge Pigeon; Squadda* or *Squatter Pigeon.*

General color light brown in varying shades.

Released on Maui and Lanai from Australia in 1922. Not likely to have survived. Cayley says: "Very similar in habits to the Squatter Pigeon." The birds received on Lanai came as Squatter Pigeons which is *G. scripta.* The name "squatter pigeon" comes from their habit of squatting for concealment.

Unfortunately I neglected to take descriptions of the consignment which came to Lanai when I was there. The birds were released but all disappeared except the peaceful dove *(Geopelia placida)* which flourished for 6 years and then disappeared.

RUDDY GROUND DOVE

Oreopelia montana (Linnaeus)

I think I saw one of these birds on Maui, at Mr. Ward Walker's place, in 1936. It was on the lawn and its general plumage seemed a ruddy shade. It seemed a short thickset bird compared with the common doves. Introduced from San Francisco to Maui in 1933. Native of Tropical America.

BLUE GROUND DOVE
Leptotila verreauxi Bonaparte

Introduced from San Francisco to Maui in 1933. Native of tropical America. I have no information as to its survival.

WONGAWONGA PIGEON
Leucosarcia melanoleuca (Latham)   Plate 16, Fig. 5

Upper surface slaty, wings darker; below white; black markings on flanks and slaty on breast.
Introduced from Australia in 1922 to Maui and Lanai. Disappeared on Lanai.

BLUE-HEADED QUAIL DOVE
Starnoenas cyanocephala (Linnaeus)

Crown of head blue, with a black border and white stripe across below the eye. The throat black with a white border.
Native of Cuba. Introduced in 1928, but evidently not established.

NICOBAR PIGEON
Caloenas nicobarica (Linnaeus)

Native of Nicobar Islands, north of Australia. Brought from Australia to Maui in 1922 and Kauai in 1928, but apparently did not survive.

PSITTACIDAE   Parrot Family

SULPHUR-CRESTED COCKATOO
Kakatoe galerita (Latham)   Plate 18, Fig. 2

White. Crest and tail sulphur yellow. Length about 20 inches.
Native of Australia.

ROSE-BREASTED COCKATOO
Kakatoe roseicapilla (Vieillot)   Plate 18, Fig. 3

Upper parts gray and white; below and neck rosy red; belly white. Length about 15 inches.
Native of Australia.

RED AND BLUE MACAW

Ara macao (Linnaeus) **Plate 18, Fig. 5**

Brightly colored with red and blue. Length about 36 inches.
Native of tropical America.

TOVI PARRAKEET

Brotogeris jugularis (Muller)
Other name: *Beebee Parrakeet.*

General color bright grass green, yellowish green below. Length about
9 inches.
Native of Central America.

INDIAN GREEN PARRAKEET

Psittacula krameri (Scopoli)

Bright green above, shading in parts; below yellowish green; a rose-
colored collar around the back and sides of the neck. Length about
16 inches.
Native of India.

Individuals of these various species of parrot-like birds have been seen
from time to time as escapees from captivity, but none of them have
become established.

PALE-HEADED PARRAKEET

Platycercus adscitus palliceps Lear **Plate 18, Fig. 4**
Other name: *Blue-cheeked Parrakeet.*

According to Caum, a pair was released by Captain Makee in 1877.
They stayed in the vicinity till one chick was raised and then took to
the woods. In 1928 I spent about a week in the Olinda forest and saw
the birds several times, and took a specimen for the Bishop Museum. I
saw them once or twice in the evening coming in from the open country
to the forest.

Many years ago, about 1895, I heard Mr. H. P. Baldwin talk of this
bird which I understood to be fairly numerous. He said it came to the
cornfields when the corn was ripe and fed on the grain.

SHELL PARRAKEET

Melopsittacus undulatus (Shaw)   Plate 18, Figs. 1, 6-9

Other names: *Grass Parrakeet; Love-bird; Budgerygah.* (This last name is spelled in a number of ways, all easily recognizable as variants of the same word.)

In the wild bird, the head and wings are yellow above, the body green, the wings and body with scale-like markings, but selective breeding in captivity has produced a number of color phases, several of which are shown in the plate.

Native to Australia, it is a favorite cage bird. Escapes are common, but the species has never become established. Either conditions here are not favorable for it in the open, or more likely pairs have never succeeded in reaching places where they could find sufficient of their proper food and make themselves at home. It is very difficult for a bird that has been hatched and raised in captivity, where food and shelter are provided, to survive very long in the wild unless it is freed in an exceptionally favorable location. Single birds have been known to travel long distances, but they usually seek the human companionship to which they have been accustomed, as for instance one bird, which escaped from its cage in the Makiki district of Honolulu, alighted three days later on the shoulder of a soldier at Wailupe, some five miles distant in a direct line. It had evidently been unable to find sufficient food, and was so weak that, despite the care given it, it succumbed that same night.

ALAUDIDAE   Lark Family

MONGOLIAN LARK

Melanocorypha mongolica (Pallas)

"Upper parts brown streaked with black; crown of head and neck chestnut, a light patch in the center of the crown; a broad white eyebrow . . . a creamy buff band around the nape . . . white on the wings; under parts white . . ." (Caum.)

Native of eastern Siberia and northern China. Introduced to Kauai by Mrs. Dora Isenberg and well established there.

SKYLARK

Alauda arvensis (Linnaeus)   Plate 19, Fig. 11

Head, plumage above mixed buff and brown; underparts lighter; breast flecked with brown on a darker surface; bill and legs brown; claw of hind toe .62 inch long; total length about 7 inches.

Introduced early from England and New Zealand. It had been formerly introduced to New Zealand from England. It became well established on all the islands, but its range has been disturbed by the growth of pineapple and cane fields. I collected several specimens on Lanai for the Bishop Museum in 1925 but I could recognize no difference between these birds and those I knew in New Zealand in the eighteen-eighties.

The skylark is not a frequenter of trees. It is a bird of the open pastures. It sings on the wing, singing as it mounts over one spot till high in the air. It descends still singing till not far from the ground, when it drops like a stone and then strikes off obliquely close to the ground. It is a beautiful singer and an acquisition on any open country. In New Zealand the skylark became somewhat of a nuisance by taking fresh sown grass seed and grain. It is adept at pulling up the sprouted seed after the plant is above the ground, and poisoned grain was resorted to, to keep their numbers down. Notwithstanding the damage they did, these small birds were a godsend to New Zealand, when invaded by grass caterpillars in the past.

The nest is a neat hollow in the ground lined with grass leaves and stems. Three or four speckled eggs are laid, varying in size and markings, some with a thickly spotted ring around the large end. Nest and eggs are almost invisible on the ground surface. When children we took pleasure in feeding caterpillars to the gaping chicks.

JAPANESE LARK

Alauda arvensis japonica Temminck and Schlegel
Japanese name: *Hibari.*

A native of Japan, introduced in 1934. It has not become established.

PARIDAE   Titmouse Family
JAPANESE TIT

Parus varius varius Temminck   Plate 19, Fig. 7
Japanese name: *Yamagara.*

Head and throat cream-colored and chestnut and bluish gray above.
Introduced from Japan at various times between about 1890 and 1928 and well established on most islands, penetrating deep into the forests. It is an entertaining little bird coming to the mountain houses and demanding food and scolding with vigor if not attended to. Broken nuts put out for it are carried off and hidden when it returns for a fresh supply.

From what I have seen of it feeding in the forests it will likely help to take the place of some of the vanishing native birds in destroying forest insect pests.

TIMELLIDAE   Babbling Thrush Family

CHINESE THRUSH

Trochalopterum canorum (Linnaeus)   Plate 19, Fig. 10
Other names: *Spectacled Thrush; Hwa-mei.*

"Length about 8 to 9 inches, the sexes alike. Plumage a rather uniform reddish to olive brown; a white line around each eye and extending backward to the ear . . . tail long and broad." (Caum.)

Native of China. Supposed to have escaped from captivity in the fire of 1900 when it was a cage bird of the Chinese. It has become well distributed and common, but in some places it seems to be receding. It had penetrated into the forests deeper than any other introduced species. Possibly the introduction of other foreign birds of late years and competition from these may have induced it to keep to the deeper woods. It is a fine strong singer and is missed from places it has apparently deserted. It frequented cane fields and when the fields were being cut, numbers were concentrated in the last patch in the middle of the field and often caught by the laborers. I have been told that it cannot spread from one island to another, and that in flying across a bay it tires and falls into the water. However, those observed may have been young birds. It is a bird of the underbrush and when disturbed flies downward and thus can be distinguished from the Hawaiian thrush which flies upward into the trees.

COLLARED THRUSH

Garrulax albogularis (Gould)
Other name: *Brown Thrush.*

Mostly olive brown above; cheeks and throat white; belly orange rufous; outer tail feathers tipped with white. Length about 11.5 inches.

Native of the Himalayan region. Introduced from San Francisco to Kauai, 1919. Established on Kauai.

PEKO THRUSH

Dryonastes chinensis (Scopoli)
Other name: *Black-throated Laughing Thrush.*

Head and nape slaty blue; above olive brown; tail feathers tipped with black; cheeks black and white; throat and fore neck black; abdomen olive brown; bill black, legs brown. Length about 11 inches.

Introduced from California to Kauai in 1931, Mrs. Dora R. Isenberg gives the information that it is increasing there. Native of south China and adjacent regions.

PEKIN NIGHTINGALE

Liothrix lutea (Scopoli)   Plate 19, Fig. 6
Other names: *Japanese Hill Robin; Babbler; Sochi-cho.*

Above olive green; throat and breast yellow; below mixed olive green and yellowish; wing varied with yellow, orange, crimson and black.

Native of south and west China. Imported here in 1918 and 1920 and established on most islands. It is a fine songster and has penetrated deep into the forests. Unfortunately it has proved to be a carrier of bird malaria. I quote from Paul H. Baldwin, Senior Foreman (Wildlife) CCC, at the Hawaii National Park in his report to the Superintendent, dated August 2, 1941, regarding bird malaria which was "discovered in blood smears from birds in Hawaii National Park in 1938 and 1939 by the writer and Donald P. Abott." The malarial parasites were identified in the laboratories of the U. S. Fish and Wildlife Service.

"The ecological implications of this discovery may be far-reaching. In the first place, the cardinal fact that bird malaria is present in the Hawaiian Islands is established. While it cannot be stated with certainty that *Plasmodium* was not present in the native bird population before the practice of introducing and liberating perching birds from other parts of the world was started, the fact that what is considered to be *Plasmodium vaughani* has been reported from the babbler in Japan is a strong indication that infected birds were at one time imported to these islands. In the second place, it shows that, while there are no records as to mosquito hosts which serve as vectors for *P. vaughani* mosquitoes capable of transmitting this parasite are present on the islands."

168 *Birds of Hawaii*
MIMIDAE   Mocking-bird Family

MOCKING BIRD

Mimus polyglottos (Linnaeus)   Plate 19, Fig. 9

Upper surface generally grayish; below whitish, grayer on the breast; outer tail feathers marked with white, inner black. Bill slightly curved at tip. Length about 10.5 inches.

Introduced from the mainland in 1928. Established on Oahu and probably on other islands. I saw it on Maui and I think on Hawaii in 1936.

MUSCICAPIDAE   Thrush, Warbler and Flycatcher Family

JAPANESE RED ROBIN

Luscinia akahige akahige (Temminck)
Japanese name: *Komadori.*

Male: Upper parts reddish olive; neck and throat brown; under parts gray, lighter on abdomen. Female duller. Length about 6 inches.

Brought to Oahu from Japan 1929-'32. Established on Oahu.

KOREAN ROBIN

Luscinia komadori komadori (Temminck)
Japanese name: *Akahige.*

Very similar to the above, but with black on the throat and breast. A native of Korea, introduced to Oahu in the 1930's, but not known to be established. It may be noticed that there are discrepancies between the technical names and the Japanese vernacular names of these two robins. Apparently Temminck, who described both species at the same time, intended to use the vernacular names as technical names, but got his labels mixed.

DYAL BIRD

Copsychus saularis prosthopellus Oberholzer   Plate 19, Fig. 14
Other name: *Magpie Robin.*

Introduced by Mrs. Dora B. Isenberg in 1922 and by the Hui Manu in 1932, but not known to be established.

SHAMA THRUSH

Kittacincla macroura (Gmelin)   Plate 19, Fig. 12

Most of plumage glossy black; patch above tail white; tail black, outer feathers tipped with white; bill black; legs pale pinkish.

Introduced to Kauai in 1931, and seemingly well established.

JAPANESE BUSH WARBLER

Horeites cantans cantans (Temminck and Schlegel)
Other name: *Uguisu.*

Top of head and shoulders greenish; upper parts brown and black; below yellow in varying shades. Length about 5.5 inches.

This bird was released by the Board of Agriculture and Forestry in 1929, by the Hui Manu and others later. I heard it in 1935 on Puukana in the Waianae mountains, and on the Niu trail. Its call and song are very distinctive. It seemed to be at home in these drier forests.

JAPANESE BLUEBIRD

Muscicapa cyanomelana Temminck   Plate 19, Fig. 8
Other names: *Blue Niltava; O-ruri-cho; Japanese Blue and White Flycatcher.*

Upper parts blue in different shades; tail black, white and blue. Bill black; throat and breast black; abdomen white. Length about 6 inches.

Native of China, Japan, Malay, etc. Introduced from Japan to Oahu in 1929, but apparently not established.

WILLIE WAG-TAIL

Rhipidura leucophrys (Latham)   Plate 19, Fig. 13
Other names: *Black and White Flycatcher; Shepherd's Companion.*

Plumage above black, below white. Length about 7.25 inches.

Introduced from Australia to Oahu, to combat flies on stock. It does not seem to have succeeded in establishing itself. I saw one near Koko Head in 1937.

PRIONOPIDAE   Wood-shrike Family

MAGPIE LARK

Grallina cyanoleuca (Latham)   Plate 19, Fig. 15
Other name: *Peewee Lark.*

Black and white in well defined markings. Length about 11 inches.

Introduced from Australia to Oahu and Hawaii in the 1920's. It feeds to some extent on pond shellfish and it was thought it might be effective in holding in check these hosts for a stage of cattle liver fluke. There are native birds which feed on these molluscs whose increase might be encouraged to this end.

STURNIDAE   Starling Family

MYNAH

Acridotheres tristis (Linnaeus)   Plate 19, Fig. 16

Hawaiian name: *Piha 'e-kelo*, probably from its cry.

Head and neck blackish; breast, sides and upper parts brown; wing barred with white; bare patch behind eye orange; bill and legs yellow. Length about 7.5 inches.

Introduced from India by Dr. William Hillebrand in 1865, to help in keeping down various insect pests. It destroys a certain amount of fruit, sometimes interferes with other birds' nests, makes a great noise on its roosts and was blamed for spreading the seed of lantana which was at one time a great weed pest, but taking the mynah from every view point it does a great deal more good than harm. It is often said that this bird was in great part responsible for the decrease in the native birds. It is my opinion that it has had very little to do with that. Birds imported in recent years and bred in the haunts of the mynah multiplied greatly.

Young mynahs fallen from the nest have made interesting pets when taken up and cared for.

This bird is often accused of being quarrelsome but it is not more so than many other birds. Pairs fight for nesting sites, both males and females apparently taking part. They have spectacular ring fights when two fight in the middle of a ring of applauding spectators. The object of this fight has not yet been fully studied.

ZOSTEROPIDAE   White-eye Family

WHITE-EYE

Zosterops palpebrosus japonicus Temminck & Schlegel   **Plate 19, Fig. 5**

Other name: *Mejiro.*

Upper surface green; white ring round eye; throat yellow; below light brown and gray. Length 4.5 inches.

Introduced from Japan to Oahu in 1929. It increased rapidly and spread to Lanai and probably other islands without assistance.

This is a favorite cage bird with the Japanese, who use it in singing competition. A young chick fallen from a nest was taken into a home and placed in a cage near a screened window. Its chirp brought a number of adult birds each carrying an article of food, an insect or a caterpillar; they climbed on the screen trying to reach the one in distress and when it was placed outside they fed it. This seems a remarkable trait in these birds. The young bird became very tame, but eventually escaped.

Japanese have told me that the birds raised on these islands are better singers than the imported birds.

The white-eye is a useful bird, though it eats a certain amount of fruit it also consumes large numbers of noxious insects and their larvae.

As the breeding season approaches the male white-eye whistles his sweet little song early in the morning. Each has an area along the highway about a quarter of a mile apart. The song is light but very sweet. The nest is neatly suspended from between several twigs.

It is not strange that this little bird should spread from island to island. A bird of the same genus, *halmaturina* came to New Zealand in 1856, no doubt from Australia or Tasmania. Apparently they came in large numbers, a flight of over 1,000 miles. It was one of the first birds with which I became acquainted.

PLOCEIDAE   Weaver-bird Family
STRAWBERRY FINCH
Amandava amandava (Linnaeus)   Plate 20, Figs. 3 & 4

Male in breeding plumage: mostly crimson, marked with ashy brown, tail blackish; wings brown. Female: above brown, crimson on upper tail-coverts, tail like the male; breast ashy brown. Length about 4 inches.

According to Caum this bird was an escapee from cages and established itself on the lowlands around Pearl Harbor, Oahu. It was restricted to this locality and had not spread much. When on Maui in 1936 I searched for some that were reported to be in a valley in the Kula district but I did not find them. Its home is in southeastern Asia.

RICEBIRD
Munia punctulata topela Swinhoe   Plate 20, Figs. 5 & 6
Other name: *Spice Finch.*

Above light brown, streaked with faint buff; throat chestnut; breast gray with chestnut markings; belly whitish. Length about 4 inches.

Introduced, it is supposed, by Dr. Hillebrand about 1865. It became very numerous on all the islands, and was much of a pest in the rice fields. But now as little rice is grown, it has become an entertaining wayside bird. It has a peculiar fluttering flight, flying backwards with ease. One will alight on a grass head, bend it down with its weight to the ground when its companions will gather around and feed on the seed. A young bird from a fallen nest made a lovely house pet. It is an extremely friendly bird, and enjoys the company of the human members of the family.

Its nest building is an interesting study. A favorite material is the flower heads of the garden pampas grass or grass leaves. These are cut from the plant as with a knife. They are packed together into an oval-shaped ball with the space for the nest in the center and a round entrance hole in one end. It undoubtedly glues the leaves together till set in position, as otherwise they would not hold together. The finished nest is quite a compact structure.

JAVA SPARROW

Munia oryzivora (Linnaeus)   **Plate 20, Figs. 12 & 13**

General plumage gray; head black and white; rump and tail black. Length about 6 inches. A pure white form is occasionally seen in aviaries.

An early introduction but did not become established. Native of Malaya.

ENGLISH SPARROW

Passer domesticus (Linnaeus)   **Plate 20, Fig. 7**
Other names: *Sparrow; European House Finch.* Hawaiian name: *Manu liilii* (the little bird).

Male: Above chestnut and light brown; below ashy. Length 6 inches.

An early introduction, before 1870. It was established when I arrived in 1890 but has not increased to any appreciable extent. Here it is a quiet bird and does little or no harm. In New Zealand it was a noisy and a cheeky one, the males especially. The mynah on the other hand has not increased to any extent in New Zealand in the last 55 years.

Without the hard English winter to keep down its numbers the sparrow increased enormously in New Zealand and became a pest in the grain fields, but could be kept in check by poisoning. It no doubt did a great deal of good as it fed its young on caterpillars. In Hawaii the sparrow is more common around the dairy ranches and the chicken farms, but in the cities it feeds gratefully on food thrown out for other birds and on what table scraps it can find, hopping in and out among the mynahs and Chinese doves and not interfered with by either. The three old time species make a very harmonious group, which is not joined by any of the more recently imported birds.

The nest is a mass of grass leaves and stems with a hole in the side and a chamber in the middle. It is put in any place it will stay. In New Zealand the large tufts of *Astelia* which filled many tree tops furnished them fine nesting places. It was interesting to see them at a grain stack. The sheaves were placed with the grain head in and the "butt" out so the birds could not get at the grain without pulling out the straws. The bird would seize a stem of oats and fly backwards pulling the long straw till the "head" was out and it could feed on the grain.

ICTERIDAE   Oriole Family

MILITARY STARLING

Troupialis militaris (Linnaeus)

Above brown with black markings; throat, middle of neck, breast and upper belly scarlet; red in front of eye and on bend of wing. Length about 10 inches.

Native of Chile and southern Argentina. Introduced from Washington to Kauai in 1931. I was told of it being seen when on Kauai in 1936.

WESTERN MEADOW LARK

Sturnella neglecta Audubon

Easily recognized by its yellow breast and black crescent on throat; and its habit of throwing up its tail as it alights on the top of low shrubs, showing the white feathers. Length about 9 inches. Its flight is peculiar. It is a fine singer.

Introduced from California to Oahu and Kauai in 1931, to Niihau in 1934, to Maui also about that time, they seem to be established only on Kauai. I saw one probably of this lot at the head of the Waikolu Gulch, Molokai in 1936 where it seemed at home on the sparsely brush-covered land. Native of western North America.

I watched this bird with much interest on the borders of the open land near Mrs. Dora Isenberg's Kilohana residence, where it is well established. I noted its call note, its song and fluttering sailing flight.

FRINGILLIDAE   Finch Family
CARDINAL
Richmondena cardinalis (Linnaeus)   Plate 20, Figs. 9 & 10
Other names: *Kentucky Cardinal; Red Bird.* Hawaiian name: *Ulaula.*

Male, mostly red; red crest on crown; female, gray above; dull red on wing and tail; below buff. Length about 8 inches.

Introduced since 1929 and now well established on Kauai, Oahu and Hawaii, it is a favorite bird at the feed trays in Honolulu. A beautiful but ungallant bird, he feeds alone in the feed tray and drives the female out if she comes in, but relaxes occasionally to take a grain out to her as she sits on a twig near by. I have seen the female trying to enthrall the male by showing her less bright colors but he seemed as indifferent as the females of other birds assume to be when the male is showing off.

BRAZILIAN CARDINAL
Paroaria cucullata (Latham)   Plate 20, Fig. 11
Other names: *Brazilian Crested Cardinal; Red-headed Cardinal.*

Above gray; underparts white; head, crest and throat scarlet.

A very beautiful bird. Introduced to Oahu in 1928 by Mr. William McInerny and well established. Mrs. D. R. Isenberg imported some to Kauai which are increasing. In contrast to the other cardinal the male and female feed together side by side in the feed tray.

POPE CARDINAL
Paroaria larvata (Boddaert)

Head crimson, crest small; upper plumage dark gray. Differs from the Brazilian cardinal in small crest and less red on the breast. Length about 7 inches.

Introduced to Oahu by the Hui Manu in 1931, but it does not seem to have found conditions favorable to it.

NON-PARIEL BUNTING
Passerina ciris (Linnaeus)   Plate 19, Figs. 1 & 2
Other names: *Butterfly Finch; Painted Bunting.*

Upper parts blue green and reddish, below red. Female green above, yellowish below. Length about 6 inches. Not known to be established.

Native of south-central United States, Central America to Panama.

INDIGO BUNTING

Passerina cyanea (Linnaeus)   Plate 19, Figs. 3 & 4
Other name: *Indigo Bird.*

Male blue; female olive-brownish above, white underparts. Length
about 5.5 inches. Not known to be established.

Imported in 1934 from San Francisco. Native of south Canada and
the United States.

CANARY

Serinus serinus canaria (Linnaeus)   Plate 20, Figs. 14 & 15
Hawaiian name: *Manu mele.* (Literally, the singing bird.)

Many canaries escape from cages but from generations of care and
confinement they are not adapted to care for themselves and guard against
enemies in the open except in rare cases. One such case is Sand Island
of the Midway Islands. For many years the Commercial Pacific Cable
Company allowed no dog, cat, rat or even mouse to land on the island.
Mr. Daniel Morrison was in charge there for 15 years and Mrs. Morrison
lived there with him for 9 years. The Morrisons brought several lots of
tame canaries to the island and bred them there. They released eleven.
These at first made their nests in the grass but later took to building them
in the ironwood trees, which also had been introduced. It was their habit
to come to the house demanding food and I believe they still come to
be fed at the houses. Some think they also feed on the seeds of the ironwood trees. Mrs. Morrison informed me that these canaries were the usual
yellow birds when released, though some had a few dark feathers mostly
about the head. According to recent informants these birds breeding in
this semi-wild state have changed color. Some are almost pure white,
some brownish and there are many intermediate grades. This is an interesting fact showing evolutionary changes from changed conditions in a
comparatively short time. It would add to the interest if the dates of
release were available and a set of specimens taken at the present time.

LINNET

Carpodacus mexicanus frontalis Say   Plate 20, Fig. 8
Other names: *California House Finch; Papaya Bird.* Hawaiian name:
Ai-nikana. (Literally, the papaya eater.)

Male: above brownish gray, red on forehead, throat, breast and rump;
gray and brown on belly. Female is without the red. The males vary a

great deal perhaps in different stages of age, although a not uncommon color phase shows orange in place of the red or reddish pink. A full-fledged male is a nice looking bird.

An early introduction, probably by escape from captivity, and well established over the islands, especially near grass lands. It is a nice singer, friendly and trustful, sometimes building its nest and raising its young in hanging pot plants on the verandah or porch by the door of a dwelling. Its food is mostly grass seeds, so it is most numerous on certain grassy lands.

Besides the birds enumerated the Hui Manu has imported in recent years the Butterfly or Mexican Bunting, Sun Birds, Narcissus Flycatchers, and others which have not become established. The Butterfly Bunting was brought by air just before the start of the war.

Index

Index

CHANGES AND CORRECTIONS IN SCIENTIFIC NAMES OF BIRDS

Since the first appearance of this book in 1944, there have been a number of changes in the scientific classifications and names of the birds described. With the publication of the revised edition, the author has taken advantage of the opportunity to include the following list of new names and to correct several errors in the earlier nomenclature.

p. 21. Wedge-tailed shearwater: Puffinus pacificus chlororhynchos Lesson.

p. 41. Hawaiian goose: Branta (nesochen) sandwichensis (Vigors).

p. 42. Hawaiian duck: Anas platyrhynchos wyvilliana Sclater.

p. 44. Laysan duck: Anas platyrhynchos laysanensis Rothschild.

p. 64. Hawaiian tern: Anous tenuirostris melanogenys Gray.

p. 80. Nihoa miller bird: Acrocephalus kingi Wetmore.

p. 80. The elepaios are classified as Muscicapidae or Muscicapinae—old world flycatchers.

p. 83. Kauai oo: Moho braccatus (Cassin).

p. 85. Molokai oo: Moho bishopi (Rothschild).

p. 86. Hawaii oo: Moho nobilis (Merrem).

p. 87. Oahu oo: Moho apicalis Gould.

p. 96. Apapane: Himatione sanguinea sanguinea (Gmelin).

p. 100. Kauai amakihi: Loxops virens stejnegeri (Wilson).

p. 101. Hawaii amakihi: Loxops virens virens (Gmelin).

p. 102. Maui amakihi: Loxops virens wilsoni (Rothschild).

p. 102. Molokai amakihi: Loxops virens kaalana (Wilson)—now considered the same as Loxops virens wilsoni.

p. 102. Lanai amakihi: Loxops virens chloroides (Wilson)—now considered the same as Loxops virens Wilsoni.

p. 103. Oahu amakihi: Loxops virens chloris (Cabanis).

p. 104. Green solitaire: Loxops sagittirostris (Rothschild).

p. 105. Kauai creeper: Loxops maculata bairdi (Stejneger).

p. 106. Olive-green creeper: Loxops maculata mana (Wilson).

p. 106. Perkins' creeper: Paroreomyza perkinsi (Rothschild) is now thought to be a hybrid between Loxops maculata and Loxops virens virens.

p. 106. Molokai creeper: Loxops maculata flammea Wilson.

p. 107. Lanai creeper: Loxops maculata montana (Wilson).

p. 108. Maui creeper: Loxops maculata newtoni (Rothschild).

p. 108. Oahu creeper: Loxops maculata maculata (Cabanis).

p. 116. Kauai akialoa: Hemignathus procerus Cabanis.

p. 118. Hawaii nukupuu: Hemignathus wilsoni (Rothschild).

p. 122. Dysmorodrepanis: Dean Amadon includes Dysmorodrepanis munroi Perkins under Psittirostra psittacea (Gmelin).

p. 124. Psittirostra deppei Rothschild is also included under Psittirostra psittacea (Gmelin).

p. 125. Palila: Psittirostra bailleui (Oustalet).

p. 126. Hopue: Psittirostra palmeri (Rothschild).

p. 127. Rhodacanthis flaviceps Rothschild: Psittirostra flaviceps (Rothschild).

p. 128. Telespiza: Psittirostra cantans cantans (Wilson).

p. 129. Laysan canary: Psittirostra flaviceps (Rothschild).

p. 130. Nihoa telespiza: Psittirostra cantans ultima (W. A. Bryan).

p. 130. Chloridops: Psittirostra kona (Wilson).

p. 133. White-faced glossy ibis: Plegadis guarauna (Linnaeus).

p. 134. Black brant: Branta nigricans (Lawrence).

p. 136. Baldpate: Anas (Mareca) americana (Gmelin).

p. 136. Gadwall duck: Anas strepera Linnaeus.

p. 137. Lesser scaup duck: Aythya affinis (Eyton).

p. 138. Canvasback: Aythya valisineria (Wilson).

p. 138. Greater scaup duck: Aythya marila (Linnaeus).

p. 140. Wilson's snipe: Capellagallinago delicata (Ord).

p. 145. Western belted kingfisher: Megaceryle alcyon caurina (Grinnell).

p. 148. Prairie chicken: Tympanuchus cupido pinnatus (Brewster). To this should be added the lesser prairie chicken: Tympanuchus pallidicinotus (Ridgway).

p. 171. Ricebird: Munia nisoria (Temninck).